# IN and OUT of TUNE

# Also by Robert Ponsonby

*Musical Heroes: A Personal View of Music and the Musical World Over Sixty Years*
Giles de la Mare Publishers Ltd, 2009
ISBN 9781900357296

**Front cover photos**
(top) 1981, London. William Glock, John Casken, Peter Maxwell Davies, RP, Nigel Osborne, Simon Rattle.
(bottom) 1975, Tokyo. Hilary Groves, Charles Groves, Pierre Boulez, RP

# IN and OUT of TUNE

## A light-hearted look at a serious life

by

## Robert Ponsonby

DIADEM BOOKS

# IN and OUT of TUNE
## A light-hearted look at a serious life

Published by Diadem Books

For information, please contact:
Diadem Books
8 South Green Drive
Airth, Falkirk.
FK2 8JP
Scotland UK
www.diadembooks.com

ISBN: 978-1-326-53663-3

*To*
*Jay*
*with love and*
*thanks for laughter*

# CONTENTS

# Introduction

This is not the book I first planned because, in May 2014, I lost the only typescript of a dozen or more chapters of my memoirs – from birth to about 1987. The lady who had typed them had very recently bought a new computer, so the 'back-up' was gone. Their disappearance remains unexplained – and seems inexplicable. But, unless some miracle occurs, they are lost for ever and, because I couldn't possibly try to rewrite them, this is a different kind of book: more anecdotal, more atmospheric and – I hope – more amusing.

Basically chronological, the book has a number of diversions. These occur when any particular activity (for example, Teaching and Talking) or association (e.g. Royals) spans a number of years. I hope the reader finds them diverting. I also hope that he or she may have read my earlier *Musical Heroes*, which, in a limited sense, is complementary to this book.

As to its title, my dear friend Mickie Rose (who has a nice turn of wit) suggested *A Tall Story*, making my great height its focal point. But – amusing as it was – I felt it would have given the wrong impression: I would like to be taken as an averagely truthful person.

*In and Out of Tune* was finished during the summer of 2015 and where I have referred to ongoing matters – for example, the future of the BBC – it will be out of date. So I must ask the reader to accept what I say as a snapshot of a particular moment.

That last sentence was written on the morning of 10 September. Later the same day BBC TV transmitted the recording of an extraordinary event. In the vast rotunda of the Royal Albert Hall we heard and saw an American musician of Asian origin playing all the six Suites for solo cello by Johann Sebastian Bach, one of the very greatest of 'western' composers. The achievement of Yo-Yo Ma was astonishing: he played from memory, his technique and intonation immaculate, his performances beautifully shaded by subtle *rubato*, his stamina prodigious. And his self-evident humanity was rewarded not only by a very big and very attentive audience (no intrusive photo-flash or mobile-ring) but also by marvellously unobtrusive camera work: we often watched his left hand at what seemed like impossibly close quarters.

The whole event was flawlessly achieved – and inspiring. I shall always think of it as a golden example of the world of performance art which I have experienced at close quarters for many years. And I hope that this book may entice some newcomers into that wonderfully moving and pleasurable world.

# 1

## Early Days

I was born on 19 December 1926 and christened in Christ Church Cathedral, Oxford, where my father, Noel, was organist. My family was almost excessively Anglican. My father's father was a Canon, my mother's father a Bishop. A great-uncle was Bishop of Gibraltar, whose diocese covers the Mediterranean, and of whom I like to think it is true that when he paid his courtesy visit to the Pope, the pontiff remarked, "I believe I am in your diocese." Much later, an uncle became Dean of Canterbury. So I grew up in an aura of Anglican sanctity.

When he died on 10 December 1928, my father was 37 – and I was barely two, so I do not remember him. Many years later, the Dean of Christ Church gave me permission to install a stone to his memory on the floor of the north transept of the cathedral. In Cumbrian slate, it is very simple. There is a more elaborate and colourful memorial in Escot Church, near Ottery St Mary, where my father's sister, Felicity Kennaway, lived.

On my father's death, my mother and I moved to Ely, where her father was the Bishop (and where my parents had met, my father then the organist). We lived in the Bishop's Palace – a very large (and very cold) house, later to be a Sue Ryder home, later still a part of the King's School. The episcopal establishment was considerable: a chaplain, of course, and a small chapel, a butler, a chauffeur and two gardeners. In the big garden there was, there still is, a tremendous plane tree. The family name was White-Thomson

3

and my mother, Mary, had three brothers – Charlie, an Eton 'beak'* killed descending from the Piz Roseg with three other beaks in 1933; Walter, killed in North Africa early in the war; and Ian, later to be Dean of Canterbury. 'The uncles' were fun. They played an indoor game, known as 'fug', which simply meant keeping a rubber ball off the ground by kicking it. The Bishop, gaiters and all, joined in very dashingly and I remember the four of them careering and whooping round the Palace's hallway. More seriously, the uncles played precipitate eight-handed 'duets' with their mother on the two upright pianos in the drawing-room – Mendelssohn and Tchaikovsky I seem to remember.

In due course my mother married again. Leslie Jaques, like my uncle Charlie, an Eton beak, had, as a very young soldier, earned an M.C. Though not at heart a military man, he later commanded the Eton College Officers Training Corps – to my acute embarrassment when, in 1944, I became a senior member of it. In any case my home – after a brief spell when my mother and her new husband were relieved of my presence and I stayed with my paternal grandparents in London – was now in Eton. The house, 'Ballards' in Keate's Lane, was where my brother, Nigel, himself in due course an Eton beak, and my sister, Celia, were born. News of Celia's birth was relayed to me at my prep school – Newlands, Seaford, Sussex – whither, at the age of eight or so (and apparently the only boy *ever* to arrive wearing 'long trousers') I had been sent. It was a good school, if not a *very* good school. The music teacher, a Miss Fox, sometimes played to musical boys on Sunday evenings. Her party piece was Chopin's Fantasy-Impromptu, which I loved and thought phenomenally difficult. Thank you, Miss F., for instilling in me a lasting love of Chopin's music.

More momentously important was my first visit to Glyndebourne, on 2 June 1938. I was the guest of the mother of

---

* Eton-speak for 'master'

4

the Stutchbury twins – boys in the school whose home was on the Downs near the Cuckmere valley and whose family were enlightened patrons of music and musicians. The opera was *Don Giovanni*, Fritz Busch of course the conductor, the cast characteristically international, the Don, John Brownlee, Australian, the Leporello, Salvatore Baccaloni, Italian – as was the Ottavio, Dino Borgioli. The Austrian Elvira, though, was not the advertised singer, Luise Helletsgruber, who had fallen ill, but her compatriot, the eminent Hilde Konetzni, who stepped in at very short notice (as she did when Lotte Lehmann as the Marschallin broke down during *Rosenkavalier* at Covent Garden).

Though the performance enthralled me, I cannot pretend that I took away a cogent recollection of what I had heard (and seen). I *think* I remembered Brownlee's top A in the final scene, but I was not yet ready to understand the miracle of Mozart's ensembles, those in *Don Giovanni* (*Figaro* notwithstanding) surely unsurpassed, musically and psychologically, anywhere in opera. I have always thought Fritz Busch a wonderful Mozartian and it did not bother me that he used a piano for the accompaniment of recitatives: I didn't know any better.

*Don Giovanni* was later to play an important part in my musical life. And *much* later I was to ask Thomas Beecham why – so far as I knew – he had never conducted the work. His reply was fascinating – and, to me, surprising: "Too difficult, dear boy, too difficult." Surely, I thought, he was almost uniquely equipped to interpret this masterpiece. His glorious recording of *Die Zauberflöte* (made with the Berlin Philharmonic in 1938) was of course a different cup of tea – a German *singspiel*, with Masonic overtones, its sexual implications, unlike those in the *Don*, innocent, almost childish. But the recording was the occasion of one of my favourite Beecham stories and one not very well known. He was a guest at an official reception when a senior Nazi asked him whether he was satisfied with the quality of the Berlin Philharmonic. "Oh yes indeed," said Beecham, "the orchestra is excellent – but have you heard the *Bournemouth* orchestra?"

With the coming of war in 1939, I moved on from Newlands to Eton, having sat and failed a scholarship. I found myself in the 'house' of Harry Babington Smith, a kindly, rather straight-laced bachelor, and it was tacitly understood that I would 'forget' that my mother and stepfather lived round the corner.

# 2

## At Eton

An early mathematics report reads:

> He spends so much of his time playing the piano when he
> should be doing Mathematics that he cannot get a great deal of
> consecutive teaching. For one labouring under this handicap
> he has done creditably; he always takes pains, but sometimes
> gets out of his depth when trying to fathom a problem.
> I have nothing but praise for his attitude (apart from the
> open contempt he shows for the subject by walking out on me
> once a week).

The writer of this nicely ironic document was A.E. Conybeare,
later to be Eton's Vice-Provost.

I did indeed spend a lot of time playing the piano, one of
my teachers being Thomas Dunhill, whose light opera *Tantivy
Towers*, with a libretto by A.P. Herbert, had had a successful
London run in 1931. Another teacher was a Mr Beswick, who
was later to teach Thomas Beecham's stepson, Jeremy Thomas.
("God help you, sir," said Sir Thomas, when introduced to
him.) Neither was inspiring – but I make no excuses for my
very modest achievements on the piano. Nevertheless, because
standards were low, I managed to win the School Music Prize
and to play the slow movement of the Beethoven C major
Concerto at the School Concert in March 1944. (The two long
runs towards the end of the movement went well and Dunhill,
conducting, 'caught' me efficiently.) Another slow movement,
from Mozart's D minor Concerto, had been played a year

7

earlier by Hugh Wyndham, a duet-partner who was a better pianist than I was and who had to cope with the fast middle section of his concerto movement. He had also played Chopin's *Berceuse*, which I loved and often attempted (almost always breaking down during bar 39), at a School Concert – a hazardous undertaking before a probably restless audience, most of them looking forward to bawling out Joseph Barnby's two School Songs, a ritual not unlike the Last Night of the Proms.

But Hugh had strong nerves – and double-jointed fingers. We had a lot of fun playing Saint-Saëns's Variations on a Theme of Beethoven and the less demanding of Brahms's 'St Anthony' Variations. And he was good company, with a whimsical degree of detachment from the realities of life. Friends with whom he had stayed reported that his suitcase had contained only a toothbrush and one gym-shoe. Other musical friends included Robert Goff, who played yet another slow movement, that from Beethoven's C minor Concerto, and who was to become an eminent judge; Simon Streatfeild, later principal viola in the LSO and later still a busy conductor in Canada and Scandinavia; and Jeremy Thorpe in Beethoven's Second Romance, of whose performance I can find no review, though in a Music Competition the College *Chronicle* reported that, "Thorpe played his solo with great spirit and effect; but his choice might have been better suited to his technique." I think I know what the reviewer meant.

The *Chronicle*, a four-page (sometimes eight-page) periodical which was just what it said it was, is now a beguiling Memory Lane. But throughout the war its first feature was invariably a list, often not very short, of Old Etonians who had been killed. Other regular features covered sport, of course, and music. Its editors at the end of the war were a future Governor of the Bank of England, Robin Leigh-Pemberton, and Mrs Thatcher's Cabinet Secretary, Robert

Armstrong. They – and previous editors – sometimes asked me to review concerts by visiting recitalists and I recall writing about Clifford Curzon and Cyril Smith, whose immaculate performance of the Brahms Paganini Variations was an eye-opener: I realised I had no hope of ever playing that well. As well as music reviews, the *Chronicle* sometimes printed creative pieces – celebratory, often parodic, poems and light-hearted essays. The editors must have been short of reportage when they agreed to print my jejune essay on Bathrooms, which is nevertheless reproduced at the end of this chapter.

Wartime Eton was not, of course, immune from hazards and deprivations: powdered eggs and 'reconstituted' potato linger tastelessly on my palate. An enormous hutch teeming with rabbits was meant to provide us regularly with meat, but I do not recall many, if any, bunny-meals. In 1940 two smallish bombs landed on the school, perhaps aimed at Windsor Castle. One demolished half of the house of the much-loved Henry Ley, Eton's Precentor, while he was eating supper in the other half. The second turned out to be a time-bomb which had fallen on a corner of School Yard. In due course it went off, doing a good deal of damage and shattering much of the undistinguished Victorian stained glass on the north side of College Chapel. This time Ley's role was more active: he was asked to make an immense noise – with forearms and feet – on the Chapel organ (a five-manual instrument) so that broken fragments of glass were brought tinkling down. Some time later the glass was replaced. In the east window a magnificently colourful creation by Evie Hone was flanked on north and south sides by very sympathetic designs – two a side – by John Piper, the remaining windows filled with 'plain' glass which was actually very subtly coloured.

In due course Ley taught me the organ – not on College Chapel's splendid instrument (a Hill), but on the less grandiose organ of Lower Chapel, where I had for a time donned a surplice and sung in the boy-based Chapel Choir, which was, I fear, not a patch on the choir in College Chapel. This was part of a professional choir school which was later disbanded, Eton, by way of compensation, establishing the Music Scholarships which proved to be the springboard for its now astonishingly high musical standards.

But the Eton I knew was not all music and journalism. There were academic requirements – and sport. As to the former I will say no more than that I am truly grateful to have been taught Latin and Greek and so to understand the sources of our language. Without a classical education it must be impossible to make rational sense of words like tele-vision, bio-graphy, sym-phony or, for that matter, dia-rrhoea. But good, systematic English is in any case being mutilated by the internet and 'textspeak'. Sport was another matter. Rather late in the day I was awarded my house colours for doing not much more than charging around energetically in Eton's own peculiar Field Game. And for obvious reasons I represented the school at the High Jump. But I clearly remember Eton being comprehensively thrashed by Leighton Park School, a smaller and much less grand establishment, in an athletics match.

On half-holidays boys were required to take exercise – either a formal game or a run – and this no doubt burned up at least some of the energy seething in teenage men. Part of it, of course, took the form of libido and this could be gratified in private or, perhaps, during the kind of horseplay which I guess was not uncommon, curiosity – as well as pleasure – playing a large part in the goings-on. I suppose some boys were 'queer' (the word then used) but we did not know – and did not much care: we were not, as today seems to be the case, obsessed by sex.

In my earlyish teens I contracted mumps and, years later, discovered that I was sterile. But I was glad to be able to echo Ian Wallace, who had had TB in his private parts and who I once heard say, "I am infertile but not, thank God, impotent." Unaware of my condition, it did not therefore bother me. But a constant, small, nagging worry was the possible length of the war and, hence, the risk of my being involved in military action.

The sensible reader will skip what follows.

## Bathrooms

Of all the rooms in a modern house, the bathroom most lends itself to exciting effects of decoration. When every resource of such mundane artisans as the electrician, the plumber, the sanitary engineer and the ablutionary designer has been brought into play, the bathroom, instead of becoming a room with amenities for washing, changes into something infinitely mysterious and ethereal.

Concealed lighting everywhere reveals an infinity of subterranean greens, and caerulean blues. Viewed through a warm steam, mirrors tell of a chamber of submarine proportions; taps become starfish, sponges are transformed into gorgeous anemones and, over all, bath-salts breathe the tang of flying spray and curiously delicious seaweed.

There is no doubt that such pretentious bathrooms do exist – perhaps some are even equipped with telephones and radiograms: but we have not entered their portals. No, the bathroom with which we are most familiar is a much more simple affair. It is rather white and its fittings are chromium-plated, and though, round the walls, there runs a frieze of seagulls or fishes which brings in a mild atmosphere of Brighton beach, in the corner stands a weighing-machine, symbol of more homely matters. Here we call a plug a plug – not a sea-horse. However, even in this bathroom there is one object of mystery to the guest – a small white wall-cupboard, with a mirror let into the front of it. While he waits for the water to run

11

he is attracted irresistibly towards this and he has soon opened it. The results are never very exciting: bottles of gargle and medicine, marked "To be taken in water three times a day after meals," jars of ointment and grease, a pencil of iodine, a rusty razor and many rusty razor-blades meet the eye. And now his bath is ready, so he turns away and forgets the cupboard. The bathroom has yielded up its dingy secret.

Just as there are many types of bathroom, so, though less obviously, there are many occupations for which the bathroom provides the setting. Countless people imagine that these sanctuaries are for the purpose of washing only, but they have missed some of the most delightful moments of their lives if they have never attempted to achieve the pleasures of sleeping, reading and singing in the bath. Of the first of these it must be admitted that there is an element of risk of death by drowning if the bather does more than merely drowse. Perhaps the habit should be restricted to day-dreaming, for which the gentle steaming heat of the bath is admirably suited. The second is more satisfactory in that it is much less dangerous; indeed, the only danger arises when the bather, absorbed in an all too gripping novel, forgets to regulate the temperature of the water and contracts a severe cold.

However, the most enjoyable, by far, of these three bath-time pursuits is the last one – singing in the bath – for apart from any aesthetic pleasure that the bather may derive from it, it is the only one that may be combined with the primary object, namely washing. Bathrooms, for some esoteric reason, have the most superb acoustic qualities: singers with small voices find that their volume is enormously increased, while robust voices produce a positively orchestral effect. Nor is singing in the bath confined to singers. Another reason for singing *en bain* is that it leaves no doubt that the bathroom is occupied: this is especially useful in bathrooms without locks on their doors. It also furnishes an excuse to angry requests to the occupant to "hurry up": the reply is a simple one, "I'm so sorry, I must just finish this aria: we're almost at the climax," and completely refutes the maxim that "He who baths first, baths fast."

We must not overlook, however, the part that the bathroom has played in history or, at any rate, the history that has been made in bathrooms. We get the impression that in Roman times suicide in the bath was an almost monthly event. Perhaps this is an exaggeration, but it is certainly true that a number of prominent Romans decided that the most pleasant way of putting an end to their unpleasant lives was to slit their veins while lying in a bath of warm water. History does not relate whether they wore green spectacles while doing so. Marat had the ill-luck to be murdered in his bath, and by so doing gains our sympathy, for if a man expects privacy anywhere at all, it is in his bathroom that he looks for it. What is more, to murder a man in his bath is to hit him when he's down.

Samuel Pepys achieved history by merely going to Bath and having a bath.

There is no denying that the bathroom is a place full of romance and interest; it may be large or small, pearly-white or pea-green, mirrored or tiled, and may have seen wonderful happenings – but still, at the back of the mind of the regular bather there lurks the feeling that "The Bath's the Thing."

[REVIEWS. – *The Bathers' Quarterly:* "He has wonderfully caught the spirit of the sponge." *The Times:* "… wet …" *Punch:* "The bath's on him." *Classical Annual:* "Ablutionarily frivolous." *Poetry and Art:* "All the bathos of the bath is here." *Etoniana:* "Ponsonby at his most pungent."]

First published in *Eton College Chronicle*, No. 2687 (Friday 27 October 1944)

# 3

# Royals

In the autumn of 1944, near the end of my last year at Eton, two invitations came across the river from Windsor Castle. The first was to a performance, in the Waterloo Chamber, of a pantomime, *Old Mother Red Riding Boots*, 'devised by Princess Elizabeth, Princess Margaret and Hubert Tanner'. My memory of the show is cloudy: it was pleasant, if a bit prim. But both princesses sang and acted prettily. So that to maintain that H.M. is wholly unmusical is simply not the case. That she is known now to prefer horses to Handel is no disgrace. And the second invitation surely confirms her interest in singing, if only temporary.

I was invited, with my mother (an alto), to join a party of royal friends and Eton connections to sing part-songs under William Harris, organist of St George's Chapel. And this we did, transferring to Buckingham Palace when the war was over. Once, Harris found he had left some vital music behind and I was despatched to the entrance to fetch it. The corridors were long and, en route, I encountered the Queen. "Are they in full blast yet?" she enquired, absolutely on the ball. At a later session, straining for a high note, I snapped off the back of the dainty crimson and gilt chair I was sitting on. The singing stopped and Princess Elizabeth turned and remarked, "Never mind – we'll send you the bill." She never did.

My next encounter was in Edinburgh in 1956. She was by now our Queen and, with Prince Philip, she came to the opening of the Festival, the tenth, and my first as Director.

There were, of course, elaborate formal ceremonies and Thomas Beecham conducted Beethoven's 'Choral' Symphony on the opening Sunday. At the end I led him and his wife, who though evidently unwell, managed a stable curtsey, to introduce them to the Royal couple. Next night, at the Assembly Hall, I met Prince Philip who, characteristically, suggested – apropos the performers – "I suppose you have to keep all these people in order."

After a long gap, I was summoned in 1985 to 'Buck House' to receive a CBE from Queen Elizabeth. Accompanied by my wife, Lesley, and a god-daughter, Rebecca, and very nearly prostrated by stage-fright, I just made it to her kindly presence, where she said, "I'm very glad about this." Then, "Are you still at the BBC?" And *then*, to my utter astonishment, "It's been a very long time, hasn't it?" There was a small twinkle in the royal eye and I had not the smallest doubt that she was recalling the singing forty years before – though she had no notes and was not prompted. From that moment I became an even more passionate Royalist.

Nearly twenty years later still, in 2004, I wrote to the Master of Her Music, Sir Peter Maxwell Davies, and suggested a festival celebrating the great Anglican cathedral choral tradition. Max liked the idea and there was a meeting at the flat of Judy Arnold and her husband Michael. Judy had efficiently managed the practicalities of Max's career but Michael, it was later discovered, had embezzled a very large amount of his money. He went to prison – and Judy faded into the background. But Ian Ritchie, a colleague of Max's in Scotland, headed our planning group and Carol Butler joined us as our administrator. Buckingham Palace was consulted – and the message came back that the Roman Catholics must be included. Ah well, I thought: so be it. And of course, had the project turned out to be solely Anglican, we would have been deprived of the music of James MacMillan. Initially we planned the celebration for 2009, anniversaries of both Purcell, born 1659, and Handel, died 1759. But fund-raising very soon became problematic. In one respect we were successful: we invited Subscribers to 'adopt' a particular choir, their subscription of £600 effectively paying for the appropriate number of copies of what turned out to be *Choirbook for The Queen*. There were in the end over fifty individual Subscribers, among them the singers Janet Baker and Felicity Lott, the conductors Colin Davis, Mark Elder and Jane Glover. Memorial Subscriptions were made by Charles Groves's family and by me, in memory of my father. Unexpected Subscribers were the (Tony) Blair Family. Of immense value was a multiple contribution from the Friends of Cathedral Music, whose Chairman, Peter Toyne, became a key figure in the planning of the Choirbook which in effect celebrated the sixtieth anniversary of the Accession.

But the project only safely took off when our fund-raiser, Penny Jonas, landed a six-figure grant from the Foyle Foundation. Penny (who also contributed, in one of her financial papers, an enchanting typo – 'Choirboy for The Queen') was therefore an essential part of our machinery, as was Carol Butler, who dealt with eighty choirs, fifty or so Subscribers, the Canterbury Press (who produced the Choirbook), the Foyle Foundation, and BBC Radio 3, who were, through *Choral Evensong*, very helpful. The Choirbook itself contained (in two volumes) forty-four anthems by living British composers, twelve of them specially commissioned. We 'launched' it in Southwark Cathedral at a special service – a Festal Evensong – on St Cecilia's Day, 22 November, 2011. The occasion was friendly and relaxed: there were many musicians in the congregation and the anthem was a setting by Max of a poem by Rowan Williams, the Archbishop of Canterbury. The Address was given by Lucy Winkett, earlier Precentor at St Paul's Cathedral, at this time Rector of St

James's, Piccadilly, who said, "Today is the past we will one day look back to and we hope that this contribution to the development of church music will be sung for many years to come."

A specially bound and inscribed copy of *Choirbook for The Queen* was presented to Her Majesty in 2012 at a Maundy Thursday service in York Minster.

# 4

## Soldiering

When, early in January 1945, I joined the Scots Guards as a conscript, I had grown to the height of 6 foot 6 inches and, as a consequence, was invariably right marker on parade. I was generally known as 'Lofty' (and later, at Oxford, sometimes 'Organ-Lofty') and I was accustomed to the frequent enquiry, "Say, mister, is it cold up there?" and once, much more wittily, "Say, mister, is it true there's snow on your 'ead all the year round?" John Kentish, during rehearsals of *The Trojans* at Oxford in 1950, referred to me as 'Mount Everest'.

Great height has serious disadvantages: not enough leg-room in theatres, concert-halls, planes and buses; the unavailability, off the peg, of clothes and shoes that will fit; the danger, too often not avoided, of banging one's head on low doorways or overhead beams; and, psychologically, the impossibility of not being noticed by those one is anxious to avoid. Advantages are few, perhaps the only one, also psychological, being the ability to look down on anyone of whom, for intellectual or moral reasons, one is in awe.

But in the army – particularly in the Brigade of Guards – height was no handicap. My three-year career was undistinguished, a rumour that I was to win the Sword of Honour at the passing-out parade I thought ridiculous, if flattering. My commission, as 2nd Lieutenant, came in the autumn of 1945 and my duties thereafter were mainly in London, sometimes at Windsor, occasionally in some far-flung part of Wales or Devonshire. In Wales my soldier-servant, on the morning after his first free evening, reported that it had been enjoyable. "Yes, sorr, *very* enjoyable: the Welsh girls, sorr, *very* passionate!"

My own social life, if not very passionate, was very agreeable. I was a young Guardee, so likely to be 'eligible'. Though the European war was only just over, the Season was getting going and 'debs' were around in large numbers – not all of them irresistible. I was lucky to fall in with a group, its female members apparently sometimes interchangeable, who were certainly not 'flappers', but intelligent and interesting. Often the evening would end in a night-club, Churchill's and The 400 special favourites. But what a contrast to today's 'clubs'! They were small, quiet and intimately lit, the music often provided by a pianist whose mastery of the mood was ideally suitable and whose repertoire of 'requests' limitless. As the night wore on, lights got lower, music softer and – no doubt – more sexy, the dancing couples doing not much more than prop each other up at very close quarters. But once, I remember, we went on to the home of one of us and read Shakespeare until breakfast time.

In the autumn of 1946 I was posted to the regiment's 2nd Battalion, then stationed in Hamburg. With a brother-officer, Michael Hughes-Hallett, we sailed from Harwich, our fellow-passengers two or three hundred German prisoners-of-war returning home. Mike and I were 'in charge' of them but, not surprisingly, they were no trouble and we saw little of them. At Bremerhaven we disembarked and found our way to the battalion's quarters in Wandsbek, a suburb of Hamburg. Even a short ride in a jeep after dark was enough to reveal the appalling devastation Allied firebombs had caused. The occasional glimpse of surviving civilians (we are said to have killed more than 30,000 in a few days) was disturbing: they were gaunt, yellow, wretched. I wondered where they lived – in the cellars of wrecked houses, I had to suppose: there was not much left standing. Our quarters, though, were pleasant enough, food was plentiful, if unvaried, and liquor was absurdly cheap. The contrast was pointed and very uncomfortable. Some years later, Colin Davis told me he had had similar feelings when he first went to conduct in Dresden, a much more beautiful city than Hamburg.

The redeeming feature of my Hamburg posting was opera. Astonishingly, two opera houses were active. The auditorium of the Staatsoper had been destroyed, but the iron safety curtain had saved the very large stage and here there was room for modest productions, an orchestra pit and an audience of two or three hundred. The other theatre, known as the Garrison Theatre, was bigger and undamaged. The great Günther Rennert was in charge, Hans Schmidt-Isserstedt the principal conductor. During November of 1946 I went as often as my quite modest soldierly duties allowed. I recall with pleasure a *Figaro – Figaros Hochzeit*, because everything was sung in German – an *Italian Girl (Die Italienerin in Algier)* and a *Don Pasquale*, all with Gustav Neidlinger in leading roles. He was also in *Hoffmanns Erzählungen* – a piece I have never much cared for. Rudolf Bockelmann, previously a regular at Bayreuth, was the Kurwenal in *Tristan*, which I heard twice in one week – an emotionally exhausting experience, somehow especially draining in the context of a Hamburg in ruins. The conductor was Eugen Jochum, a fine Wagnerian, the Isolde Erna Schlüter, an exceptional artist (if exceptionally plain) who had sung the role at Covent Garden. Also a member of Rennert's excellent company was Theo Hermann who, though on the rotund side for Figaro and despite some of Baron Ochs's role lying just a little low for him, brought such intelligence and character to whatever he did – including a lovely line in comedy – that I was not surprised to learn that he had coached Geraint Evans at about this time.

Back in London in time for Christmas 1946, the following year, spent in London and Windsor guarding the Royal Family and the Bank of England, turned out to be very rich in opera, ballet, concerts and film. In January, at the Cambridge Theatre, I saw *Don Pasquale* again – this time in Italian – with the wonderful Mariano Stabile as Malatesta. Though nearly sixty, Stabile (who had been Toscanini's Falstaff in 1921) had an irresistible stylishness and great wit. In the orchestral pit Alberto Erede ensured idiomatically Italianate playing. (The Hamburg performance seemed in retrospect heavy and humourless.) Erede was also in charge of *Barbiere* in the same theatre later that year when the Dickie brothers were Almaviva (Murray D.) and Figaro (William D.) and the Bartolo was Ian Wallace, the buffo bass-baritone, a Glyndebourne regular who once sang Don Magnifico (*La Cenerentola*) for Vittorio Gui in Rome where, he told me, he was addressed as 'Signor Vallachay'. Years later Ian became President of the Council for Music in Hospitals, with which I was then happily involved. He fitted the job perfectly: ideally caring and amusing he was selfless in the time he gave to the Council.

The autumn of 1947 brought the Vienna State Opera to Covent Garden with Josef Krips and a glorious cast of singers (though they sang even Mozart's da Ponte operas in German) – Schwarzkopf, Seefried, Jurinac, Cebotari, Gueden, Schöffler, Hotter, Ludwig Weber, Erich Kunz and Anton Dermota, the Don Ottavio who, at one performance, surrendered the role to Richard Tauber, by then within a few months of his death. I happened to be present and, though the voice was threadbare, there was no doubting the style and the breath control – which was amazing, for Tauber was to die of lung cancer. The Don that night was Paul Schöffler, but I was also to hear Hans Hotter in the role, because a *Figaro*, for which I had tickets, was cancelled and *Don Giovanni* substituted. Since Schöffler was also singing Don Alfonso (*Così fan tutte*) I think it

21

possible that Hotter stepped into the breach, for Don Giovanni was not really his role; not long afterwards I heard him often as Wotan and, in a *Tristan* with Flagstad, a really wonderful Kurwenal.

If I wasn't at Covent Garden in September of that year I was likely to be listening to Schubert and Brahms chamber music played by an amazing piano quartet – Artur Schnabel, Josef Szigeti, William Primrose and Pierre Fournier – put together for the Edinburgh Festival by Ian Hunter. And Schnabel had played several times at the Albert Hall in May, his Diabelli Variations unforgettable. In the same hall – no flying saucers then! – I heard Bruno Walter in Beethoven, Schubert and Mahler's First Symphony, the first Mahler I had ever heard. I was fascinated.

Earlier in 1947 I had seen a lot of ballet, much of it conducted by that erratically brilliant composer and author Contant Lambert. His book *Music Ho!*, sometimes perverse, always intelligent, makes a good case for looking to Sibelius as the symphonic way forward. In the pit, for ballet, he was masterly and I had heard him in the New Theatre during 1943 for the first time on 29 December when Margot Fonteyn was Odette/Odile and Robert Helpmann Prince Siegfried in *Le Lac des Cygnes*. Moira Shearer, in the corps de ballet, had a small solo in the Spanish Dance of Act 3, as she did in Frederick Ashton's *The Wise Virgins*, to music by Bach (arr. Walton), in which Fonteyn was the Bride. Very striking was Helpmann's *Hamlet*, to Tchaikovsky's tone-poem, in which his Ophelia was Beryl Grey, and Shearer a Court Lady. In a more familiar Tchaikovsky score, Fonteyn was the Sugar-Plum Fairy, Helpmann the Nut-Cracker Prince, Beryl Grey a Fairy.

Four years later I heard Lambert in de Valois's *The Rake's Progress*, with very pretty decor by Rex Whistler, Massine's own *Le Tricorne* to Falla's music and decor by Picasso, and Ashton's *Symphonic Variations* set to César Franck's orchestral score with piano solo. I thought it then – and think it now – a glorious masterpiece. Franck is constrained (thank goodness!) by the variation format, so we are spared his slithering chromaticisms, and the choreography is abstract. There are six dancers – three women, three men – who all need to be virtuosi: they are all very exposed. On 19 June 1947 the women were Moira Shearer, Pamela May and Gillian Lynne, the men Michael Somes, Alexander Grant and John Hart. Whenever I have seen the piece I have felt that it actually enhances Franck's score.

I never met Lambert, but I treasure his remark that Ethel Smyth – whose music he detested – "would have been the spitting image of Wagner if only she had been more feminine". (But you need to know what Wagner looked like fully to enjoy this superb joke.)

So 1947 was not, militarily, a strenuous year and on 15 January 1948 I was 'demobbed' and presented with a suit – ill-fitting and of poor material – and an unwearable hat. On 4 March I heard Furtwängler with the London Philharmonic in Mendelssohn, Mahler, Strauss and a fine Brahms First – and on 23 April I went up to Oxford, where Trinity's Organ Scholarship awaited me.

# 5

## Up at Oxford

Demobbed on 15 January 1948 and expected at Trinity College, Oxford, in April (not, because of my army service, in the autumn), I crammed the intervening months with organ practice and harmony lessons, the latter with Sydney Watson, Eton's Precentor and a striking figure: tall and lean, he was a good conductor and a minor composer (among his works a Service referred to by him as "Me in E"). That he had a pronounced stammer did not in the least hamper him, though it sometimes accorded him an accidental knighthood: S-Sydney. He was, I think, a good teacher, but I was becoming aware that I was not a gifted student: harmony did not come easily to me. Was I, I wondered, quite silly to be contemplating a degree in Music?

The problem was solved for me when on my second day up at Oxford – 24 April 1948 – I saw Jack Westrup, Heather Professor of Music, who told me firmly, but kindly, that I should not attempt to read Music. He had no doubt been briefed by Sydney Watson. That relief rather than disappointment was my chief reaction suggests that I was already reconciled to the decision, as was the fact that I had decided that English Language and Literature would be my alternative choice of subject. And my appointment as Trinity's Organ Scholar – an act of flagrant filialism (my father having had the job) – was, if it was needed, some kind of formal acknowledgement of my musical credentials.

The scholarship was, though, a very modest affair. There was no choir and only one sung service – Sunday Evensong. But the appointment was hazardous in an odd respect: the console sat on the floor of the ante-chapel, unlofted and unscreened, so that an assembling congregation passed one by within brushing distance and sometimes stopped during the retiring voluntary to observe one's pedal-work in some Bach Prelude and Fugue.

This hazard was eliminated after I had gone down: a new organ, complete with organ loft, was installed and an inaugural service arranged. I was not present, but I heard several accounts of the unhappy accident which engulfed the occasion. The organist was Ken Andrews, of New College, the doyen of his collegiate profession – who better? But Andrews had the misfortune to die in mid-service. There was an awful noise as he collapsed across the manuals and the service petered out. Brave men climbed the narrow spiral staircase to the organ loft and moved Andrews's tall body to a corner of the tiny space. The bravest of them played for the rest of the service. Later, telling this story at a Gaudy, I was interrupted by Michael Maclagan, a Fellow of the College, who insisted, "No, no! he played round Andrews's body."

My own tenure of Trinity's Organ Scholarship was untroubled and undemanding. From time to time I put together a choir of friends and we sang Passion music at Easter, carols at Christmas. I joined the Oxford Bach Choir and the University Opera Club, but I also took seriously my new commitment to English Language and Literature. I read *Beowulf* and, for light relief, both *Gammer Gurton's Needle* and *Ralph Roister Doister*, one or other of them the earliest surviving English comedy. I attended the lectures of David Cecil and C.S. Lewis, the latter surprising me because, having read only *The Screwtape Letters*, I had pictured the author as a small, decrepit bookworm, whereas he was in fact big and robust, positively pork-butcherly in appearance. I am grateful to him for the Preface to *Paradise Lost*, which led me into the complete poem and to a passage which has stayed with me –

Men called him Mulciber: and how he fell
From Heav'n they fabled, thrown by angry Jove
Sheer o'er the crystal battlements: from morn
To noon he fell, from noon to dewy eve,
A summer's day: and with the setting sun
Dropped from the zenith, like a falling star,
On Lemnos, th'Aegean isle:...

Though the Philae spacecraft flew for ten years and landed with astonishing accuracy on a comet, whereas Mulciber simply fell for a single day and landed on a biggish island, I still find the imagery of his falling more emotive by far than the space travel of a machine, however remarkable. Mulciber was, after all, flesh and blood within his poetic ambience.

*Paradise Lost* was a relatively easy read by comparison with Spenser's *The Faerie Queene*, all six of whose long books I skimmed – or perhaps skipped – through without much pleasure. And an attempt at Shelley's *Prometheus Unbound*, though it reminded me of the nice story of Rex Whistler writing to the British Museum with an offer to bind their copy, convinced me that my limited stamina was better suited to such poems as Byron's surely perfect *So we'll go no more a-roving* (of which I feel certain there are echoes in Auden's *Funeral Blues*). As to English theatre, my experience was minimal. I had seen a number of domestic comedies at the Theatre Royal, Windsor, and, at London's amazingly enterprising Arts Theatre, Alec Clunes's Hamlet and, in Ibsen's *The Master Builder*, Frederick Valk's unforgettably powerful Solness. Even more memorable, though a tiny role, was Laurence Olivier's Shallow in *Henry IV Part 2*. But that was about all, so it behoved me to acquaint myself with much more of the best of English drama – Shakespeare, of course, in the first place.

I was lucky. I saw a lot of Shakespeare, much of it in college gardens on warm summer evenings. Three productions stand out, the earliest in June 1948: *Troilus and Cressida*, with music by Robert Armstrong, in the garden of Halifax House, Troilus the 23-year-old Russell Enoch, who was eloquent, gallant and sexy and who later had a busy career mostly in TV (he was an early member of the cast of *Doctor Who*), generally using his first two names, William Russell. A bigger 'name', like me a Trinity man, was Nigel Davenport, a rumbustious Bottom in Anthony Besch's precise and intelligent production of *A Midsummer Night's Dream* in New College garden. Nigel was always busy. At Oxford he took the leading roles in the ETC's (Experimental Theatre Club) double bill of Fielding's burlesque, *Tom Thumb*, and Chekhov's *The Bear*. He was a mainstay of the OUDS Smoker of March 1950, most memorably in *O-hello*, a skit in which he appeared as Othello, The Old Moore, with Michael Codron as Desdemona, His Almanack, and John Schlesinger as Iago. In *Vesuvius*, "a Saga", he and Codron appeared in drag as Ingrid and Anna. His range was already awesome, though during a long and very successful postgraduate career he was, if not always a Bad Guy, often a Tough Guy.

Unquestionably, though, the one never-to-be-forgotten Shakespeare production during my Oxford days was Nevill Coghill's legendary *The Tempest* in the garden of Worcester College as dusk was falling. Shakespeare tells us that the 'Scene' is "The Sea, with a Ship; afterwards an Island" and Coghill made brilliant use of Worcester's lake. Caliban emerged from an empty tank unseen on the lip of the lakeside and Alonso with his Courtiers sailed during an admittedly rather timid storm, on a richly decorated punt. But the *coup de théâtre* came at the end when Prospero, in an aside to Ariel, says

My Ariel, chick,
That is thy charge: then to the elements
Be free, and fare thou well!

At this, Ariel ran away along the side of the lake and – to our utter disbelief – across its surface, stopping to wave farewell, running back to the shore and vanishing in a firework puff of smoke. That he had run out along a platform an inch or two below the surface was, on reflection, obvious, but the breathtaking magic of the moment was not lessened.

It was Shakespeare who led me from Oxford theatre to Oxford opera. In February 1949 the University Opera Club put on Stanford's *Much Ado About Nothing*, a piece well worth reviving though, by comparison with Verdi's consummate *Falstaff*, its characterisation is pallid. But Jack Westrup – whose connection with the club went back to 1927 when, as an undergraduate, he had conducted his own edition of Monteverdi's *L'incoronazione di Poppea* – next, in 1949, chose Gluck's *Iphigénie en Tauride* and he "directed this immensely important revival with fervour and scholarship" (Desmond Shawe-Taylor in the *New Statesman*). *The Times* noted that the chorus, of which I was a member, are Scythian braves, "that undergraduates will sing and act with gusto". Well, of course: involvement in any serious attempt to master and present a great musical work will surely call for commitment, if not always gusto, and will evoke emotions which are likely to last a lifetime. So it was for me with *Iphigénie*. In Scene 3 of Act 2 Orestes is separated from his dearest friend, Pylades, and falls into a swoon. Recovering, in Shawe-Taylor's percipient words, "he mistakes exhaustion for repose" and sings 'Le calme rentre dans mon cœur', a passage accompanied, unforgettably, by a faltering, syncopated figure

28

led by violas, an effect unique in all my listening and one illustrated by Alfred Einstein in his *Short History of Music*.

I graduated from chorus member in *Iphigénie* to soloist – Narbal – in *The Trojans* a year later; from Gluck to Berlioz and, in a sense, from godfather to godson. After all, Berlioz, attending a Paris performance of *Iphigénie* and noticing that cymbals had been added to one of the Scythians' dances and trombones omitted from Orestes's recitative in Act 3 had shouted out, "Who has dared to correct Gluck?" Certainly there were trombones in Jack Westrup's orchestra for the Gluck and no doubt the orchestra for *The Trojans* was properly constituted: Westrup was a fastidious scholar as well as an immensely enterprising opera promoter. Between 1927 and 1962 he conducted, for the Opera Club, Mozart's *Idomeneo* (1947) and *La clemenza di Tito* (1952), rarities by Alessandro Scarlatti, Marschner, Verdi, Smetana and Bizet, a double bill of Stravinsky and Ravel, and premieres by living composers – Egon Wellesz's *Incognita* and Alan Bush's *Men of Blackmoor*. An amazing record. It was a pleasure to have sung for him and to have witnessed, at a last night party, his masterly improvisation on the piano of a fugue based upon *The British Grenadiers*. I *think* it was after the same party that I helped him to hoist a number of undergraduates – none of them quite sober – back into their colleges. (Did he hoist me back into mine?)

Just as my mathematics had suffered – because of my piano-playing – at Eton, so, at Oxford, did my study of English Language and Literature suffer from my constant involvement in the pioneering activities of the Opera Club (which seems now, regrettably, to be defunct). I achieved a Third – and was a little comforted by the wit (who *was* he?) who justified my placing when he said that, "a Third avoids the ostentatious flamboyance of a First, the pretentious mediocrity of a Second – and the obvious failure of a Fourth."

Between Schools and my Viva in 1950 I went to Glyndebourne as a guest of John Dalrymple, who had preceded me as President of the Opera Club and who had a temporary job on Glyndebourne's staff. While there I knocked on the door of the company's management, explained that I had just come down from Oxford and hoped to work in music as some kind of an administrator. "We'll remember your name," I was politely told, never dreaming that they would.

In February I had sung Masetto (*Don Giovanni*) for Colin Davis; in November I was to sing Narbal (*The Trojans*) for Jack Westrup. Between these very modest personal achievements I was lucky enough to hear a number of supremely accomplished and moving performances by some of the best opera singers and conductors of the day: at Salzburg, Lisa Della Casa's Countess and Paul Schöffler's La Roche in Strauss's elegant conversation-piece *Capriccio*, which Karl Böhm conducted; Julius Patzak's Male Chorus in Britten's *The Rape of Lucretia*, paired with Boris Blacher's *Romeo and Juliet*, both conducted by Josef Krips and directed by Josef Gielen, father of the admirable Michael. At Edinburgh, Sena Jurinac, as Cherubino, was beginning to beguile us and Thomas Beecham stole all the available thunder in the first version of Strauss's *Ariadne auf Naxos* – as did Victor de Sabata at Covent Garden in Verdi's *Otello*. Ramon Vinay – the best Otello around till Plácido Domingo came along, reversing Domingo's shift from tenor to baritone by starting his career as a baritone – had the young Renata Tebaldi as his Desdemona. But it was de Sabata's demonic release – *allegro agitato e fortissimo* – of the opening of the opera, the Chorus and Orchestra of La Scala at thunderous full stretch, that blasted its way into my memory as one of those moments. It came on 14 September 1950.

Of the four performances of *The Trojans* (sung in French, so *Les Troyens*) given between 29 November and 2 December, the second was recorded on 78rpm discs, which was lucky for me because it was the one night on which I got right my tricky first entry – "J'ose à peine annoncer la terrible nouvelle" – a happy accident which I later recalled when the tenor Nigel Douglas told me that in a production of Janáček's *The Makropulos Case* he had for once got right a much more awkward passage and Anja Silja had whispered, "Was ist los? Das war richtig." ("What's wrong? That was right.").

The Opera Club was recorded that autumn in another way. With Richard Kent, a good strong bass who was for two years its Treasurer, I wrote 'A Short History' of the Club, 1925–50. Published privately in October, it is a review of the first 25 years of a society whose repertoire was strikingly original. I was (I am) pleased with it and later in the autumn, presumably pleased as well with my performance on stage, I enrolled as a student of singing with the Guildhall School.

But my career as the tallest bass-baritone in the business never materialised: Glyndebourne had remembered my name and just after Christmas a phone call invited me to join the organisation immediately.

# 6

## Sussex and Scotland

The 1951 Festival of Britain, a nationwide celebration, more a 'cheer-up' than a 'wake-up' call, was marked all over Sussex in all kinds of ways, some highly professional – Elisabeth Schwarzkopf with Gerald Moore in Worthing, Tito Gobbi in Eastbourne, Solomon and Myra Hess in concertos at Brighton – some self-evidently amateurish but often admirably ambitious.

Glyndebourne, whose own season was exceptionally star-studded, had agreed to provide an administrative element so as to give the county's multifarious contributions, the Festival of Sussex, some kind of central coherence. And it was in this unscripted role that I was cast. Talk about the deep end!

But I found, on reporting to Glyndebourne's Lewes office on New Year's Day, 1951, that discussions had begun about a theatrical treatment of *The Four Men*, Hilaire Belloc's picaresque account of a walk through Sussex by 'Myself', The Sailor, The Poet and Grizzlebeard (the old Belloc). The book – apparently one of his own favourites – had been adapted as a tiny ballad operetta by Eric Duncannon (a remote Ponsonby kinsman of mine), whose cousin David, a composer and piano pupil of the great Alfred Cortot, had written the music.* The cast of five, with a very small chorus, was directed by Robert

---

* Caught in Paris when the Germans invaded in 1940, David Ponsonby escaped to unoccupied France, joined the Resistance and was awarded the Croix de Guerre for his work as an interpreter.

Speaight, who played 'Myself' and who knew Belloc personally. Ian Wallace (for once not singing at Glyndebourne) was The Sailor and Eric Duncannon, a Sussex resident himself, was the narrator. A few days before the first night in Chichester on 19 May some of us lunched at Belloc's home in West Sussex. At 80 rather shrivelled and detached, he nevertheless delighted us by breaking into song, his voice a light tenor, towards the end of lunch – not one of the half-dozen songs composed by David for *The Four Men*, but a French folksong. Afterwards, over liqueurs, which he clearly much enjoyed, I explained to him what we were up to and he seemed pleased, if not wholly comprehending. But we were glad to have his implicit blessing.

*The Four Men* was a success, playing in nearly twenty towns and villages as well as four schools – Lancing, Christ's Hospital, Roedean and Steyning Grammar. Ian Wallace had doubted the viability of a project which on paper looked folksy and parochial, but in his memoirs (*Nothing Quite Like It*) admitted, "How wrong I was." I had kept an open mind, not least because of the involvement of three Ponsonbys – a musician, a theatre man and an administrator.

Though I had the grandiose title of General Secretary, my role mainly consisted of editing and producing the Festival's souvenir programme and reporting to the Festival Committee of which Glyndebourne's John Christie was a member. Since many of the Festival's innumerable events – sport, flower shows and carnivals among them – ran themselves, my work dwindled. But it so happened that Ian Hunter, who had, in 1950, 'inherited' the Edinburgh Festival from Rudolf Bing, was looking for an assistant. I was appointed, so far as I know without advertisement or competition, and I worked simultaneously for Moran Caplat (Glyndebourne) and Ian Hunter (Edinburgh). This was easy and convenient because the two bodies shared the same London office in Baker Street. (It is not generally understood that it was Glyndebourne which persuaded Edinburgh to promote an international arts festival – hence Rudolf Bing's brief time as CEO of both organisations.)

The five years which followed were an ideal apprenticeship. In 1952 Glyndebourne launched its Festival Society – in effect a body of Friends – and published its first Programme Book. I was appointed Secretary of the former and Editor of the latter. Membership of the Festival Society afforded priority booking and this privilege turned out to be almost unmanageably attractive, given the small capacity of the theatre until its inspired rebuilding in 1994, more than forty years after my own involvement. But while the theatre developed – and for the very first time acquired really good acoustics – the Programme Book's format has hardly changed in more than sixty years. The first cover was by Oliver Messel, a Peter Pan figure who designed *Idomeneo* (never before given professionally in Britain) as well as, later, more Mozart, some Rossini and some Strauss. Everything he did was enchantingly pretty, but rather predictable. Later designs by Osbert Lancaster, Leslie Hurry and Hugh Casson gave Glyndebourne's sets and costumes more weight and, in Osbert's case, more wit – the period portraits in Act 2 of *Falstaff* included recognisable likenesses of at least two members of Glyndebourne's staff. (And it was Osbert who, noticing that Eric Duncannon had had a rather cushy war, dubbed him Eric Shuncannon.)

As for Edinburgh, I shadowed Ian Hunter, first visiting that dramatically beautiful city with him in July 1951 for the monthly meeting of the Festival's Programme Committee. We took the sleeper from King's Cross to Waverley Station where, in years to come, I was to meet and greet many celebrities, among them Stravinsky who, at short notice, during a Festival in which I had programmed little of his music, turned up, insisting upon the strictest *incognito* and going to ground, with his wife and a small entourage, in the Caledonian Hotel. Anxious to observe his conditions, I saw no more of him – a major frustration: he was, after all, the most important composer of my lifetime.

But my duties in Sussex and Edinburgh left me plenty of evening-time in London and, thinking back and imagining the miraculous possibility of reliving just one year of my music-life, I don't have much doubt that 1951 would be the period I would choose. Linking some of the dazzling highlights of that year was the young Geraint Evans, Second Priest and Second Armed Man in Erich Kleiber's *Magic Flute* (Peter Pears the Tamino), Nikitich in *Boris Godunov* (Boris Christoff the powerfully moving Tsar), Melot in Clemens Krauss's *Tristan* (with Flagstad – incomparable – and Set Svanholm, no Melchior, but wonderfully musical and intelligent), Second Soldier in *Salome* (with Astrid Varnay the passionate eponymous Princess), Mr Flint in *Billy Budd* (the composer conducting) and, in Beecham's gloriously human *Meistersinger*, the Night Watchman, a role traditionally leading to greater things. Beecham it was who, earlier in the year, had introduced to Britain the 26-year-old Dietrich Fischer-Dieskau in Delius's *A Mass of Life* – a performance of extraordinary sensuous beauty from a singer once briefly a prisoner-of-war in Britain. (That I never persuaded him to sing the work again is a lasting regret.) Next day, in the Ritz Hotel, Beecham offered him the role of Hans Sachs – which he wisely declined, only taking it on 25 years later.

In his memoirs Fischer-Dieskau wrote with great warmth of Julius Patzak (they had sung the *St Matthew Passion* together) and in particular of his performance in Pfitzner's *Palestrina*. And Tom Hemsley, who 'inherited' from Fischer-Dieskau many performances of the War Requiem, once told me that when Patzak came to the great monologue in Act 2, the stage staff gathered in the wings to listen in awed homage, so

35

compellingly beautiful was it. His Florestan (*Fidelio*) was of the same order. From 'Gott! Welch dunkel hier' until the joyous duet with Leonora, 'O namen-, namenlose Freude' Patzak's every phrase, every note had intense feeling. That Covent Garden's orchestra, under Karl Rankl, was not then much more than workaday seemed immaterial. I have never heard a more moving Florestan.

Another tenor, Tito Schipa, gave a farewell recital, with Ivor Newton. An incomparable stylist with an open voice, beautifully placed, he had created the role of Ruggero in Puccini's *La rondine*. He was most at home in Rossini and Mozart, with a French strand (*Lakmé, Manon, Werther*), and his recital was an anthology of such works with, unforgettably, Alessandro Scarlatti's enchanting *Violette*. Though in his early sixties, Schipa's voice was remarkably fresh, the phrasing and breath-control still immaculate.

At least as memorable was Sena Jurinac's Ilia in *Idomeneo*. Mozart's earliest operatic masterpiece, its harmonic and dramatic innovations and its vivid choral writing (surely owing something to Gluck) sets it apart from the rest of his operatic *oeuvre*. And the role of Ilia – a far cry from Cherubino and Fiordiligi, her previous Glyndebourne roles – seemed written for Sena; it brought out her unique gift for evoking emotion in her hearers – an emotion which came straight from her heart.

Sena was not in Glyndebourne's *Don Giovanni* at Edinburgh in 1951 (but Geraint Evans was the Masetto). Another singer, absolutely different in every other way, had her gift for communicating heart-to-heart. Kathleen Ferrier, her burnished contralto instantly recognisable, was not born for the stage – she sang only Britten's Lucretia and Gluck's Orfeo – but in *The Dream of Gerontius* and the *St Matthew Passion* she projected a dramatic spirituality which was irresistible (and in one respect quite at odds with her own private, Lancashire-lass earthiness). I had to miss her legendary recital with Bruno

Walter, but I found her touching in Chausson's *Poème de l'amour et de la mer* with John Barbirolli. I had first met her in 1949 when I had turned pages for her accompanist during a recital in Oxford's Town Hall: a nerve-shredding ordeal which I survived without serious accident. I last heard her on 3 February 1953, her penultimate performance – in *Orfeo* at Covent Garden. It was known that she was unwell; perhaps only John Barbirolli, the conductor, knew that she was very near to collapse.

But in 1951 Kathleen was in her prime, and she was happy in Edinburgh. Her by no means immaculate accompanist, Bruno Walter, had another commitment: he was the conductor of seven of the New York Philharmonic's fourteen concerts, the other conductor Dimitri Mitropoulos. The Orchestra had come by sea and both conductors brought with them a Vaughan Williams work – Walter the *Tallis Fantasia*, Mitropoulos the Fourth Symphony. This naturally tough work had a performance of stupendous power and conviction, enhanced, I'm sure, by the 'sound' of the Orchestra, which was perceptibly 'harder' than that of any similar European ensemble.

Mitropoulos, whom I had met at Prestwick Airport a few days earlier, was altogether remarkable. Greek-American, he had considered taking holy orders in the Orthodox church. Certainly very generous, he had, while Bernstein's predecessor with the New York Philharmonic, been given cash and sent off to buy himself a new tail-suit, but had returned without the tail-suit or the cash, which he had given to beggars encountered en route to the tailor. (This story was told to me by Bruno Zirato, then manager of the Orchestra.) But his musical gifts were prodigious. He composed: an opera, *Soeur Béatrice*, was performed when he was 24. As a pianist, he studied with Busoni. In 1930, with the Berlin Philharmonic, he stood in for Egon Petri, who was unwell, as pianist-conductor in

37

Prokofiev's Third Concerto – a handful at the best of times. And at Edinburgh he conducted from the piano the Fourth Concerto of Malipiero (whose enormous output – over 30 operas, most of them performed professionally – has vanished from the schedules of promoters and broadcasters).

Mitropoulos was happiest in music of the twentieth century (*The Times* thought his Beethoven – the Fourth Symphony – "hateful"). His memory was phenomenal: he conducted without the score (or a baton) and his rehearsals of Strauss's *Elektra* have become legendary. I found him modest and likeable. The inclusion of Bax's *Overture to a Picaresque Comedy* in one of his programmes was characteristically thoughtful.

The late autumn of my recollected year (1951) was dominated by singers and singing. In Beecham's glowing *Meistersinger*, Ludwig Weber was an unforgettable Pogner and Elisabeth Grümmer his marvellous Eva, a role she was to sing at Edinburgh next year, along with Strauss's Octavian (standing in, once, for Martha Mödl), Mozart's Pamina (sharing the role with Lisa Della Casa) and – just for good measure – Weber's Agathe (sharing with the beautiful Clara Ebers). She adorned Günther Rennert's amazing Hamburg Staatsoper whose staggering achievement – six productions in repertoire at Edinburgh's primitive King's Theatre, none of them seen in Britain before – fully justified Ian Hunter's difficult decision *not* to engage Glyndebourne, for the first time in the Festival's then brief history.

But in London, during the autumn of 1951, Grümmer sang only for Beecham and everything that I heard at that time, including the premiere of Britten's *Billy Budd*, was eclipsed, for me, by a performance of Schubert's *Winterreise* given by Hans Hotter with Gerald Moore at the Kingsway Hall. It was my first hearing of that great cycle and I blushed – I still blush – at the recollection of my own performance of its first four

38

songs at Balliol College two years earlier. Hotter's dark bass was sometimes rather too loose, but the intensity of the feelings he conveyed and his sense of the progression of that most melancholy journey were incomparable – "Fremd bin ich eingezogen…"

# 7

## My Little Eye

On 6 April 1955 I learned that I was to succeed Ian Hunter, my boss and mentor, as the director of the Edinburgh Festival. Nobody was more astonished than I was, particularly as two of my successors, George Harewood and Peter Diamand, were believed to be in the running. I had to suppose either that neither of them wanted the job just then or that the Festival authorities preferred the young devil they knew: I was not yet 30.

Determined to make my own mark, I set out on a *tour d'horizon* designed to ensure that my first festival – which was also the tenth – was memorable. I was looking for an opera company, an orchestra or two and, with luck, a theatre company, perhaps a dance ensemble. And I wanted to see Günther Rennert again: I much liked and admired him.

It was nearly ten years since, as a soldier, I had heard opera in Hamburg. Times had changed (though Rennert had not): at the Volksbühne I heard, and hugely enjoyed, *Die Abenteuer des Königs Pausole*, by Honegger from Pierre Louÿs. Part musical, part revue, part legshow, it was very topical and fast: there were digs at sex and homosexuality. And I was delighted to see Theo Hermann again, once more in a fez as the King, with the young Hermann Prey as Giglio. But at the Schauspielhaus, where I had heard *Tristan* and *Rosenkavalier*, they were playing *Das Dunkel ist Licht genug* and *Charleys Tante*. When I saw Rennert he told me he was negotiating with

Covent Garden for an autumn visit in 1956 – but that if Edinburgh's offer came first he would come to the Festival.

I went on to Frankfurt, but it was soon clear that the Städtische Oper was not ready for Edinburgh: the company was still settling down. I had a ticket for Schiller's *Don Carlos* – but was forced to surrender at the end of Act 1, which had lasted two and a quarter hours.

On the Rheinblitz train to Munich, where you can feel the mountains and where my wonderful hotel room had every possible mod con, I began to think – despite Rennert's interest – that Munich might provide me with an opera season in 1956. It soon emerged, however, that Munich's own festival – of which I had not been aware – would make an Edinburgh visit impossible. I was sorry, because, at the Prinzregententheater, I had heard a very good *Fidelio* under Eugen Jochum, with Birgit Nilsson a wonderful Leonora. I had also heard Elisabeth Lindermeier (Rudolf Kempe's first wife and a lovely creamy soprano) in *Der Freischütz*. But this was not going to work.

After a day off in Zurich, where I heard a snatch of *Die Fledermaus* at the Stadttheater, I flew on to Prague. Securing a visa had been problematic (Soviet bureaucracy had been involved) but I had an extra, non-musical job to do.

A good friend, Royd Barker, who had played oboe in my *Semele*, was at the beginning of what turned out to be an important career in the Intelligence services, when he had regular contact with the Cabinet Secretary, Robert Armstrong, and was evidently listened to, though he was discretion itself with ordinary mortals. But when, *en passant*, I mentioned to him that I was going to Prague, he pricked up his ears and I quite soon found myself in discreet conversation with one of his colleagues. Would I, this anonymous person asked, be willing to do a small job for his Service? I said I would, provided I had a cast-iron guarantee that I would not find myself locked away in some Siberian gulag. This I was promised and the nature of the 'job' explained. It had four elements, the first quite incomprehensible: I was to try to see whether, by the axles of the railway trains, there was a white box. I saw no trains. More practical was the request to try to see, on the periphery of the airport, a particular type of advanced MiG fighter. I was shown silhouettes but saw no such planes. Nor did I succeed in retaining my visa, when leaving Prague. I was staying, as a foreign VIP, at the Alcron Hotel, where it was assumed that sophisticated bugging was installed. Could I possibly find out whether a particular room on the hotel's first floor housed its nerve centre? Now, my room was *not* on the first floor, so I had no obvious need to be there, but whenever I could, I left the lift at that level and strolled nonchalantly, my heart going pit-a-pat, past the room in question. And my last day brought success: as I passed the room, its door was briefly opened and I glimpsed a bank of small lights, some of them winking.

My feeble espionage apart, I had had time to be shown – to my surprise – a lovely Canaletto of Westminster in the National Gallery and in the main cemetery the tombs of Smetana and Dvořák. I had heard the Czech Philharmonic, under Karel Ančerl, and the visiting Leningrad Philharmonic (in Prokofiev, Lyadov and Tchaikovsky) under the great Mravinsky. With both orchestras I was later to be involved when I engaged them for Edinburgh. On 25 May, I saw Janáček's *Jenůfa* at the National Opera. I had seen Charles Mackerras's *Katya Kabanová* at Sadler's Wells, but this – perhaps because I was in Prague – was an epiphany: the composer's idiom – small cells repeated cumulatively and supporting melody, the diction related directly to speech, the humanity and the concise mastery of dramatic tension were unlike any other composer's methods. And his range – from *The Cunning Little Vixen* to *From the House of the Dead* – was surely unique. Janáček was *sui generis*, his music nearly lost

(Hans Gál once explained to me) but now acknowledged as a very great man of the musical theatre. When, much later, I was directing the Proms, I included at least one of his works every year between 1974 and 1985. And in due course I was awarded the Czech government's Janáček medal during a rather stiff dinner at their Embassy.

From Prague I flew south to Milan and there, thanks to the British Council, I had one of the best theatre experiences of my life. The Piccolo Teatro – quite a young company, occupying a smallish, bright modern theatre – was managed by Paolo Grassi, but the dynamo director was Giorgio Strehler, soon to be a world name in opera and theatre. His production of Goldoni's *Arlecchino* was quite simply a miracle. He had somehow rediscovered the way to play *commedia dell'arte* and the production raced by, often *fugato presto*, with bewildering and enchanting panache. From time to time everything stopped and once – unforgettably – the stage was suddenly empty except for a blancmange, shaking silently by the footlights. When, next year, the production came to Edinburgh (with Pirandello's *Questa sera si recita a soggetto* – 'Tonight we improvise'), it stole the theatrical honours. But Marcello Moretti, who gave me a replica mask (now the property of the actor Kevin Thompson), played not only Arlecchino but also Dr Hinkfuss in the Pirandello and I'm told that his relatively early death was the consequence of the extreme strenuousness of the Arlecchino role, which he played many times.

I'm not now quite sure why I went on to Naples: I wasn't likely to find there any of the groups I was looking for. But, in the Teatro San Carlo, I heard a concert by the Israel Philharmonic. Leonard Bernstein was the conductor, the soloist Isaac Stern, in Bernstein's *Serenade*, a Stravinskyish work, "much of it", I noted in my diary, "no more than very good film music". The Neapolitan audience was in two minds: there was some booing – and some shushing of the booing.

Whereupon Stern strode onto the platform and announced, "Adagio et Fuga en Sol mineur de Bach." That quietened everybody, as indeed it deserved to.

I left Naples on 1 June, sharing a taxi to the station with an American couple who had been disappointed by the city: "My husband went for a walk," said the wife, "but he says there's nothing here." Oh, the innocence of the American tourist!

In Rome, I called on Richard Incledon, with whom I had holidayed in Italy in 1949, and who was now studying for the priesthood at the Collegio Inglese. We sat in the garden, where there was a recently installed swimming pool into which Cardinal Hinsley had made the inaugural plunge. This amazing event had been recorded by Richard on a commemorative plaque which was subsequently seen by the Oxford classics don, Thomas Higham. But, Higham said, Richard's wording implied that the Cardinal had entered the pool feet first.

Another friend, Roger Toulmin, then *The Times*'s correspondent in Paris, put me up for two nights on my way home and we heard Berlioz's *Symphonie fantastique* and Lully's *Dies irae* with the orchestra of the Garde Républicaine in a setting next to the Comédie-Française, some of whose stars could be seen leaning elegantly from their dressing-room windows.

I flew back to London on 5 June, well pleased with what I had seen and heard and with the contacts I had made. I immediately invited Milan's Piccolo Teatro to the 1956 Festival and I made sure that my offer to Rennert's Hamburg company preceded Covent Garden's.

# 8

## Edinburgh

So far as I know, only two books have been published which review the Edinburgh Festival's history and achievements.

The first, George Bruce's *Festival in the North*, is so slipshod and amateurish that it refers flatteringly to the visit of the Czech Philharmonic in 1959 – a visit that did not take place because the Czech government, whose agency had signed my contract, reneged on it when they remembered that Johanna Martzy, the foremost interpreter of the Dvořák Violin Concerto, was an expatriate. I was asked to replace her, which I refused to do, so that Martzy got her dates and our Royal Philharmonic (with Hans Schmidt-Isserstedt and Walter Susskind, born in Prague) got the Czech Philharmonic's. But the loss of that great orchestra was grievous.

The second book, by Eileen Miller, covers the Festival from 1947 to 1996 and it is a model of what such books should be – well written and full of immaculate detail. A nice feature is a series of reviews of the achievements of each festival director, beginning with Rudolf Bing (1947–9) and stopping (where the book stops) with Brian McMaster (1992–). My own review (1956–60) is as good as I could want and, that being the case, this chapter will not present a chronological account of my time as festival director. Instead it will be largely anecdotal, behind-the-scenes stuff.

I must begin with an incident which preceded my appointment as director: I was Ian Hunter's deputy and on the last night of the 1951 Festival we agreed that I would attend the performance (in the woefully inadequate Empire Theatre) by the Belgrade Opera Ballet, a company from behind the 'iron curtain'. Their last piece was an attractive blend of folk and classical, *The Gingerbread Heart*, the conductor Oskar Danon, who was beginning to record some Russian opera for Decca Records. I had organised a party for the company, which was to fly back to Belgrade early next day, and in the small hours we boarded buses for Prestwick airport on the Ayrshire coast. I was, of course, in my dinner jacket. We got there in good time and I looked for the two DC3 aircraft they needed. But only one was on the runway. My suggestion that half – about 35 of them – should go on ahead was opposed by their political 'minders' who were anxious not to split the company. But I insisted and in due course they flew off. I then learned that the second aircraft would not appear till early next day. So I found myself at Prestwick airport with 35 Yugoslavs who were going to need a bed that Sunday night. Racking my brains, I came up with what I still think a brilliant solution.

Butlin's holiday camp was not far away and, yes, they could accommodate the company – and me. We drove over in a bus and I realised that many of them had never seen the sea. We were all exhausted so went early to bed. But during the night there was discreet knocking on my door. The company's interpreter, the very pretty Dušanka Djermanović, was outside: "Mr Robert, I need your help. Two of the dancers wish to defect. What is your advice?"

I said that I did not know anything about their family circumstances; nor did I know how the Home Office would react. So I asked, please, not to be a factor in their decision. (In the event, they defected in Vienna, during a refuelling stop.) Eventually, early on the Monday morning, the second half of the company flew off, later sending me a long letter, signed by them all and illustrated by a rather good drawing of me ("Daddy Long-Legs") waving them goodbye.

*Still* in my dinner jacket, I returned to Edinburgh, where a change of clothes, a bath and a very large whisky could not make up for the sense of desolate anti-climax which pervaded the city after the last night of the Festival.

This was in 1951 and subsequent adventures were none of them so prolonged or so strenuous. But in 1956 I was faced with an odd problem. The Hamburg State Opera, our guests in the King's Theatre, whose proprietors were Howard and Wyndham, were to open their season on the Festival's first Monday with *Die Zauberflöte*, conducted by Rudolf Kempe. The Queen and the Duke of Edinburgh were to be present, so the National Anthem was called for. Imagine my astonishment when a letter from Howard and Wyndham informed me that the Anthem would be conducted by the Company's Director of Music – Geraldo! It took me some time and much correspondence to persuade them that their proposal was inappropriate, indeed preposterous. In the event, Kempe made a very good job of the Anthem and then delivered a glorious *Flute*, sometimes reminiscent of Beecham's great recording with the Berlin Philharmonic.

The problem of the Anthem did not arise when, next year, La Scala were the visiting opera company and, unavoidably but regrettably, everything they did was overshadowed by Maria Callas's supposed defection before the fifth and last performance of Bellini's *La sonnambula*. I have explained elsewhere, and not only in my earlier book, that she was blameless and I won't repeat myself. But I can't resist recalling a rebuke delivered by Callas in the King's Theatre. I had gone to see that all was well and found her rehearsing on stage with piano accompaniment. The auditorium was dark and, with my colleague, John Bassett, I slipped into a seat at the back of the stalls. Inevitably we had innumerable small problems to discuss and we were whispering, *sotto voce*. But we were audible to Callas, who stopped singing, removed her glasses

47

and having advanced to the footlights, said, imperiously, "Either you talk – or we sing." I comforted myself with the hope that she could not have seen who the whisperers were.

A few days later a small dilemma concerning Giuseppe di Stefano called for quick thinking. I had arranged three press conferences – one for the company as a whole, one for Callas and one for di Stefano. For the last I had booked a largeish room in the George Hotel but, going there in advance, I found very few journalists indeed. (Callas's had been packed out.) Conscious of the likelihood of serious embarrassment – not least for the tenor – I asked the hotel's manager if he could corral any of his guests sitting around with nothing better to do, and invite them to enjoy a glass of sherry among such real journalists as turned up. The manager saw the point and mustered quite a few of his customers, who were tickled by the deception. By asking a good many questions myself the subterfuge worked and di Stefano – a nice man and a wonderfully stylish Nemorino (in *L'elisir d'amore*) – was unaware of it.

If Maria Callas was the undoubted *prima diva assoluta* of the 1957 Festival, there was an amazing array of actors, among them Jean-Louis Barrault in Anouilh's *La répétition* and, in Jonathan Griffin's controversial *The Hidden King*, Robert Eddison, Michael MacLiammoir, Ernest Thesiger and Derek Nimmo. But by chance two important erstwhile dancers appeared – Moira Shearer in Hasenclever's *A Man of Distinction* and Robert Helpmann in Sartre's *Nekrassov*. They had already appeared together, at the 1954 Festival, in *A Midsummer Night's Dream* (with Mendelssohn's music) and in Stravinsky's *The Soldier's Tale*, and both had had major roles, Shearer the star, in the film *The Red Shoes*. Also in the film had been Anton Walbrook, now Shearer's co-star in the Hasenclever play: a complex reunion. And a reunion of huge talent. Shearer shone in good company: as well as Walbrook, the cast included Eric Porter and Prunella Scales and if, vocally, she sometimes rather lacked timbre, this was hardly surprising since dancers use every part of their bodies except their voices.

With Helpmann it was another matter. His range was extraordinary: as a classical dancer he had often partnered Margot Fonteyn, he had been the eponymous star in his own ballet *Hamlet* (to Tchaikovsky's music), and, in Laurence Olivier's glorious film of Shakespeare's *Henry V*, he had had the cameo role of the Bishop of Ely, hilariously making the most of an early scene in that otherwise earnest play. Also in Shakespeare, on television years later, he had delivered the first line of *Richard III*, but not quite right – "Now is the summer of our discontent..." For a split second his eyes betrayed desperate panic, but he got back on the rails with a second "summer" delivered with completely different colour and more emphasis. He was a witty man and I particularly enjoyed his comment on the controversial issue of nude dancing – "Not everything stops when the music stops."

Otto Klemperer had appeared at the 1957 Festival in two concerts with the Bavarian Radio Symphony Orchestra, one of them an all-Beethoven programme. With another such programme he opened the 1958 Festival, this time with the Philharmonia Orchestra. That the concert very nearly did not take place was a fact known only to me and my immediate colleagues.

Anxious that the great man should have comfortable and convenient lodgings, I had reserved for him a ground-floor suite at the George Hotel. But I did not know that he was in the grip of an impulsive obsession with a pretty string-player in the Philharmonia Orchestra whose members were staying in the University hostel in East Suffolk Road on the Southern outskirts of Edinburgh. So I was astonished when he phoned me to say that he wished to transfer from the George Hotel to the hostel – a wholly unsuitable notion, for he was 73 and had suffered from a variety of accidents and illnesses. So, feeling sure of my ground, I told him that unfortunately the hostel had no vacancy. But I did not know my Klemperer who, in a further call, told me that in fact Room 38 was available. Nonplussed, I tried hard, and failed, to persuade him to abandon his plan: our conversation was inconclusive. Next day he was to give the Opening Concert of the Festival and I went to the Usher Hall to wish him well, hoping that he might have forgotten our argument. No such luck: I was obviously unwelcome, for he threw down his walking stick and made for the Green Room's lavatory. I thought it best to make myself scarce and went to my seat, praying fervently that he would emerge onto the platform. He did, of course, and gave us a wonderfully luminous 'Pastoral' Symphony (with *The Consecration of the House* Overture and the Fifth Symphony). I thought it best not to go round to congratulate him.

The following day I was out and about most of the time but when I returned to my office in mid-afternoon I was met on the stairs by my wonderful secretary, Ruth Lachmann. She had been in tears and told me, "Doctor Klemperer is here. He is in your office. He is sitting at your desk." Indeed he was – and he greeted me: "Why are you smiling?" A bad beginning. So I sat down opposite him, the interviewee as it were, and we debated his problem, getting nowhere much. Then he said, "Send for the scales of justice" – by which he meant those pretty brass scales on which one weighed one's letters to determine the stamp-value needed. We argued, and when he thought he had made a point, he put a weight on one side; when he judged that I had scored, he put one on the other. And, miraculously, he achieved equilibrium at the moment when we agreed that he would sleep at the George Hotel, but could spend time (he said he would be composing) at the University hostel during the day. The elemental laugh which accompanied this accord signalled a permanent – and on my part an affectionate – truce. Next day he gave the Festival a compelling Haydn–Bruckner programme and prefaced it, from the rostrum, with a touching tribute to Vaughan Williams, whose death on 26 August had been announced that morning and to whose memory he dedicated the concert.

The Festival's own tribute to VW was conducted by Adrian Boult a year later. The composer's status was not then nearly as high as it later rightly became and Boult's programme (of which I am not proud) showed signs of practical convenience:

Concerto for Two Pianos
A Sea Symphony (Symphony No. 1)

The pianists in the Concerto, an unfamiliar work, were the husband-and-wife duo of Vronsky and Babin, of Russian origin and both pupils of Schnabel, who no doubt learned the work for the occasion. In the Symphony the admirable soloists were Heather Harper and John Cameron. But the chorus, critically important in the *Sea Symphony*, was the Edinburgh Royal Choral Union, self-evidently local and aurally second-rate, a choir which remained rather an embarrassment until, in 1965, George Harewood created the Scottish Festival Chorus under Arthur Oldham, a choir-trainer of international standing.

A more prominent concert of English music by a single composer was the Festival's Opening Concert, when William Walton conducted the Royal Philharmonic in his Partita and First Symphony. In his Cello Concerto the soloist was Pierre Fournier, who also gave the Beethoven Sonatas with Wilhelm Kempff – performances which I preferred to those of Rostropovich and Richter which I later heard at Edinburgh during the 1964 Festival: some of their tempi were breathlessly fast. I had admired Fournier since I had first heard him in 1947 and I now discovered in him a passion for Ealing Studios

51

comedies, surprising in an artist so elegant and aristocratic – but we laughed a lot recollecting them, as did his beautiful wife, who described herself as "une pianiste manquée".

No laughing matter was Iain Hamilton's Sinfonia for Two Orchestras, which I had commissioned to mark the bicentenary of Robert Burns's birth in 1759. I had given Iain *carte blanche* as to style, assuming that he would produce a reasonably accessible piece. But he was in a fiercely astringent period and made no concessions: the audience were gobsmacked and the Burns Foundation, which I had persuaded to share Iain's fee and which had no doubt expected a pot-pourri of folksy tunes, declared the work "ghastly". Luckily I had also arranged a number of Burns-related recitals in the Lyceum Theatre, among the performers Compton Mackenzie, by now an adopted Scot who lived in Edinburgh, though born and educated in England. Founder of *Gramophone* magazine, the range of his achievements as a writer and occasional actor was astonishing, *Whisky Galore* his best-known book (and, later, film), *My Life and Times* (in ten 'octaves', each covering eight years) his longest. But he was also a practised raconteur and I shall always treasure his story of the swimmer who, on a sunny summer afternoon, entered the water at Helensburgh (near Glasgow) and, floating on his back, fell gently asleep until... "Bump", his head encountered Mallaig Pier (getting on for 100 miles away as the crow flies, *very* much more round the coastline). "And what did you do then?" asked a friend. "I swam back." Not long afterwards I was grateful to 'Monty' Mackenzie for his support when my resignation became public.

It can't be fanciful to think that Robert Burns and John Betjeman shared certain characteristics – humanity, simplicity, brevity and a nice naughtiness. But this was not the reason why I invited John to give an afternoon reading during 'Burns year'. I had introduced such readings in 1958 when Peggy Ashcroft and Edith Evans had both given recitals in the Lyceum Theatre (where T.S. Eliot's verse-drama *The Elder Statesman* had been playing). Both had been popular, but it was time for a male poet and Betjeman was the obvious choice. His performance was a masterclass. He shuffled on to the stage, seeming to wear bedroom slippers and blinking into the theatre lights. He thanked his audience for coming "on such a lovely day" and told them he would quite understand if they didn't come back for the second half, when he would be reading his own stuff. He had them eating out of his hand.

Would that things had gone so well for my second poet, Edith Sitwell, invited not just for her status but also because of the Walton connection (though I had not managed to put together a performance of *Façade*). I have read somewhere – in an apparently authoritative source – that Dame Edith came to Edinburgh by car, but I distinctly remember meeting her on a branch line at Waverley Station when my formal enquiry about her health evoked the disconcerting response, "I have been unwell. I fainted twice last week."* A bad omen – and one disastrously fulfilled at the theatre. Her entrance, a tall black-draped sibyl, was, alas, the high point of her recital. Because her voice lacked timbre, the theatre had provided her with a mike and whether this malfunctioned or whether she misused it is irrelevant: she was more or less inaudible beyond the first few rows. And, quite soon, voices were raised – "Speak up", "Can't hear you" and so on. (The nature of her readings saved her from the double comment which Noël Coward once endured: "Louder... and *funnier!*") Then there was an amazing exchange –

Voice: "Why don't you take your face out of the book?"

E.S. (looking up): "You won't like what you see if I do."

---

* I was later reminded of Stephen Spender's comment on it being "extremely difficult to take Sitwell illnesses as seriously as they really are [because] the whole ménage is given to falling down on a scale that seems grotesque."

She ploughed on, with truly heroic courage, to a dwindling audience. I was mortified.

A week before, in the same theatre, the Old Vic had played Congreve's *The Double Dealer*, in the cast two 25-year-old actors, both, like Edith Sitwell, to become Dames – Judi Dench and Maggie Smith. How I wish I could promise, hand on heart, that I had spotted their prodigious gifts. More obviously talented were two established Swedish singers, Elisabeth Söderström and Kerstin Meyer, both stars in the versatile ensemble of the Royal Opera, Stockholm, which endeared itself to the Edinburgh public by its warmth and friendliness. Söderström sang Marie in Berg's *Wozzeck* and Ortlinde in *Die Walküre*, in which Meyer was both the Fricka and the Rossweisse (as well as Ulrica in *Un ballo in maschera* and Maddalena in *Rigoletto*). As if this was not enough she gave, with Gerald Moore, a concert for children in the Roxy Cinema. No wonder Edinburgh said goodbye to the Swedes with affectionate and tearful regret.

Glyndebourne Opera had not appeared at the Festival since 1955 and I was very pleased to find that in 1960, my last Festival, I could agree manageable terms with the company. And they did us proud, bringing Geraint Evans's incomparable Falstaff and, in Bellini's *I puritani* (Bellini not personally a favourite) the phenomenal vocal agility of Joan Sutherland. Much more interesting, in my view, was the triple bill conducted by John Pritchard which comprised works by Wolf-Ferrari, Busoni and Poulenc, whose *La voix humaine*, directed and designed by Jean Cocteau, was unforgettably personified by Denise Duval.

Conductor of the two Italian works was the genial Vittorio Gui, an absolute master of nineteenth-century bel canto opera and of *Falstaff*, which is in a different stylistic category – more Mozartian in its brilliantly characterised ensembles. Gui's compatriot, Carlo Maria Giulini, was also a guest, also in Verdi

– but in the Requiem, not opera, though he had conducted *Falstaff* at the 1955 Festival. I have to say that I found Gui's reading warmer and more witty, Giulini's rather po-faced by comparison.

Gui also had a choral concert of works by Carissimi and Rossini, the former, though prolific, now almost forgotten. The latter called for the use of an organ and at the morning rehearsal in the Usher Hall not a sound could be coaxed from the seriously neglected 'resident' instrument. I summoned professional help, but it seemed all too likely that it would not be repaired in time. Now Gui's son-in-law, the conductor Fernando Previtali (who had appeared at the Festival in 1953), was present at the rehearsal and I explained my dilemma. "You have an organist?" he asked. I said, "Yes, of course." "Allora," said Previtali, "'ave 'im *seem* to play" – a suggestion which reflected rather adversely on the acuity of his father-in-law's ear.

No controversy surrounded the conductor of the Leningrad Philharmonic, the great Evgeny Mravinsky, whose three programmes (Gennadi Rozhdestvensky gave a fourth) included Tchaikovsky's last three symphonies. The Orchestra was in superb shape, Jewish members not yet expelled, horns and woodwind very audibly 'Russian' and Mravinsky, apparently an austere tyrant, in movingly magisterial control. But I had a small personal difficulty. Going to the stage door of the Usher Hall to wish Mravinsky well – as I invariably did on any artist's 'first night' – I found my access barred by two muscle-bound thugs, Soviet 'minders' no doubt, there to protect the whole party from subversive reactionaries like myself. We had only two words in common, in my case "Da", in theirs "Nyet", and these we exchanged for quite a while until, eventually, I got my way, perhaps because, though much less muscular, I was taller than they were.

Two musicians who endeared themselves to concertgoers – and to me – in 1960 were Myra Hess, Dame Myra since 1941, and Isaac Stern. Both had concertos, but their joint recital in the Usher Hall was unusual because their programme of Beethoven, Schubert and Brahms included Howard Ferguson's Second Sonata – in one sense a foretaste of Isaac's appearance, in 1986, at Peter Maxwell Davies's St Magnus Festival in Orkney, when he premiered Max's Violin Concerto. Not only a master musician, Isaac was also a wit. It was he who unforgettably remarked, *à propos* concert audiences, that "If nobody wants to come, nothing will stop them."

Dame Myra told me a story less universal, indeed wholly personal and – just possibly – apocryphal. She was contracted to give a recital in a dim suburban place on a Sunday afternoon in February, but she awoke that morning feeling miserably unwell. Being a real 'pro', she battled out to the hall where she was to play and there asked if someone could find her a nip of brandy. But, no brandy apparently available, she was brought port, some of which, thinking "better than nothing", she swigged... with consequences which surprised even her – "I started a Chopin Waltz in 4-time." *Se non è vero, è ben trovato.*

When, in 1957, I had introduced a satirical note into the Festival programme and had invited Anna Russell to give late-night performances in the Freemasons' Hall, I had no idea where this innovation would lead. Comedy had always been a welcome ingredient in our drama programme, but satire often at the expense of the serious arts was something new – and I later learned that Sol Hurok, the grand panjandrum of American promoters, had deplored what he saw as the undermining of the work of those who promoted great music and great theatre. I could see where he was coming from for Anna Russell's *pièce de résistance* was a satirical commentary on Wagner's *Ring* cycle. But, as she had studied singing at the Royal College of Music and had been married to a horn-player, her satire was informed, subtle – and very funny. So, two years later, in 1959, I invited her back, this time to the much bigger Lyceum Theatre, where Flanders and Swann – gentler comedians – also played. Both shows sold well so, for 1960, I decided to promote late-night entertainment during all three weeks of the Festival. Least controversial were Les Frères Jacques, a small French group with a nice line in subtle burlesque: one song had as its refrain "la truite de Schubert". Uniquely and inimitably funny (also, like Anna Russell, of Canadian origin) Beatrice – 'Bea' – Lillie brilliantly sustained her solo show of quick-fire wit, of course including the famous tongue-torturing monologue about the ordering of "a dozen double-damask dinner napkins" which was spoken not into a phone, but into the flower of a large white lily. For the third week I had decided on, not comedy, but jazz, and negotiations with Louis Armstrong seemed to be going well when they collapsed – and I had a week to fill at the Lyceum Theatre.

The story of *Beyond the Fringe* has been told so many times (not always accurately) that here I will be brief.

I had often been irked by the success of undergraduate revues on the Fringe which stole too much of the thunder of the official Festival and I decided to promote such a revue – but one which would be 'beyond [the capacity/gifts of] the Fringe', a title which, to this day, I sometimes find is misunderstood. Between us, my colleague John Bassett and I knew, or knew of, the four young men who soon came to my London office and went away with *carte blanche* as to material and a manageably modest sum of money. The rest is history. Unwittingly I had, in the words of Caryl Brahms, co-author of that very amusing book *A Bullet in the Ballet*, "opened the flood-gates of satire". So, if she was right – and I've no doubt she was – I was the *fons et origo* (and once a victim) of *Private Eye*, launched in 1961: a happy thought.

57

The last day of my last Festival – Saturday 10 September 1960 – had begun on a light-hearted note when my successor, George Harewood, 'Cuckoo' under my baton in the Toy Symphony, had played one of his entries upside-down, "Oo-cuck", while, last thing that night, Peter Cook, Alan Bennett, Jonathan Miller and Dudley Moore had made a good shot of turning upside-down, with dotty illogic, some of the conventions of social custom.

I am content to be remembered by these frivolities but I hope that Festival visitors that year will also recall performances by Gioconda de Vito, Mstislav Rostropovich, Claudio Arrau and Victoria de los Angeles; plays by Chekhov, Dürrenmatt and Bjørnson; ballets by Kenneth MacMillan, John Cranko and Leonide Massine, with, among the dancers, Margot Fonteyn and Svetlana Beriosova.

As for me, I was on a Cunard Queen within a week, reflecting – when not catching up on sleep – that I was exchanging one of Europe's very grandest of arts festivals for a Caribbean caprice hardly more than a day-dream. Ah well, the die was cast. I was 'admitted' to the U.S. of A. at New York on 20 September 1960.

# 9

## "I remember it well..." – Theatre Thoughts

Happening upon the enchanting recording by Maurice Chevalier and Hermione Gingold of the duet in which, line by line, Gingold, with uncharacteristic gentleness, contradicts every single one of Chevalier's memories ("I remember it well") of a romance they had once enjoyed, I had to conclude that I *did* remember well Gingold's intimate revue, *Sweet and Low*, which ran at the Ambassadors Theatre between 1943 and 1946, developing through the comparative, *Sweeter and Lower*, to the superlative, *Sweetest and Lowest*. The show became for me a happy addiction. I loved the clatter of the two pianos which introduced it and, where needed, accompanied the sketches. I loved Henry Kendall and the actors (all of whom could either sing or dance – or both) who shared the stage. Above all, I loved Gingold, whose venomous charm and none-too-subtle innuendo have been incomparably well described by Kenneth Tynan. Two of her sketches are stuck in my mind – 'Cello solo', in which, grey-haired, bowed and bandy-legged, Gingold lamented, "If I'd only never taken up the 'cello", and 'Borgia Orgy':

> The Borgias are having an orgy,
> There's a Borgia orgy tonight,
> But isn't it sickening –
> We've run out of strychnine:
> The gravy will have to have ground glass for thickening. [...]
> When the butler flings open the dining room door

There's a cunning contraption concealed in the floor;
We wonder who'll sit on the circular saw
At the Borgia orgy tonight.

A couplet in the introduction to the final version was also worth a snigger:

New brooms sweep clean,
But yet some dirt remains.

Though without doubt also an 'intimate revue', *Beyond the Fringe*, launched at the 1960 Edinburgh Festival, was in every conceivable respect different. The four writers were the actors – and one of them provided the music. There was no scenery to speak of and few props. The words were the thing and the sketches were quite wordy. They were also highly political: Harold Macmillan was mercilessly guyed by Peter Cook in 'T.V.P.M.' (and is said to have seen the performance). 'Take a Pew', Alan Bennett's Anglican vicar's sermon, soon became a classic. Jonathan Miller's 'The Heat-Death of the Universe' was a fantasy which grew from the need of an impoverished person (the narrator) to buy a pair of trousers from the London Passenger Transport Board Lost Property Sales Department to the vision of 400 naked men, "their 800 horny feet pattering [...] through the chilly nocturnal streets of sleeping Whitechapel". These were solos. 'Aftermyth of War' (to which I can't help thinking Alan Bennett's *Forty Years On* owed something) involved all four, Dudley Moore also providing a piano commentary – Beethoven's Fifth, 'I Vow to Thee, My Country', 'Deutschland Über Alles' and a Chopin Prelude among other snippets. Dame Myra Hess, who wove "her magic fingers inextricably into the heartstrings of London", was invoked, and Peter Pears and Benjamin Britten were ruthlessly – and brilliantly – parodied in 'Little Miss Britten' – 'Muffet' being the template of the sketch.

60

Some – notably the pre-London audience in Brighton – thought parts of the show offensive and 'Aftermyth of War' sailed close to the wind, appearing to ridicule The Few, the RAF pilots who won the Battle of Britain. But Peter Cook's highly developed sense of the absurd disinfected such ridicule of any real outrage. For example,

[Squadron Leader to Flight Officer Perkins:] I want you to lay down your life, Perkins. We need a futile gesture at this stage. It will raise the whole tone of the war. Get up in a crate, Perkins, pop over to Bremen, take a shufti, don't come back. Goodbye, Perkins. God, I wish I was going too.

The person who doesn't spontaneously chuckle at that is surely quite a few laughs short of a healthy sense of humour.

Peter Cook and his colleagues maintained – not too convincingly – that satire was not their main aim, which was simply to make people laugh. In this they were gloriously successful and I remain grateful to them all (though, as I write, only two survive) for the laughter they brought to my last Festival in a city still haunted by the severe spirit of John Knox.

No such spectre troubled Glasgow, by nature uninhibited, whose Citizens' Theatre often attracted attention by its radical posture and sometimes literally unbuttoned productions. I went there as often as I could (which was not often) and I remember particularly well Peter Nichols's *A Day in the Death of Joe Egg*, one of those plays which bring laughter into tragedy – something only the theatre can do effectively. Joe Egg is a child so handicapped that its – actually her – father describes it as "a human parsnip" and its sole vocal contribution is an occasional "Aaaah!" I was alerted to this play by Andrew Leigh, whose father, Walter, a pupil of Hindemith, had had a successful composing career until his death at Tobruk in June 1942. Andrew, who then managed 'the Cits' and was later to manage the Old Vic, persuaded me to support Nichols's play, which was first performed on 9 May 1967, and I became a theatre 'angel', making a small profit on my very modest investment (£50, I seem to remember) – I was happy about this, but couldn't help wishing I had invested a similar sum in *Beyond the Fringe*.

Never mind: I remember it well... and nobody is contradicting me.

# 10

## New York, Nassau and Knightsbridge

I had resigned as Director of the Edinburgh Festival in September 1959, but had been asked to stay on to run the 1960 Festival. My decision was unavoidable, but also rash: I had nowhere to go. So a phone call from Huntington Hartford, the multi-millionaire inheritor of A&P Stores (of whom, when he called, I had never heard) was, it turned out, a lifeline, though a precarious one.

'Hunt' told me that he had bought Hog Island, near the waterfront of Nassau, capital of the Bahamas, and planned to develop it as a festival centre – initially for open-air theatre and film, later for music and the visual arts. (The previous owner, Axel Wenner-Gren, supposedly a Nazi, had, it was rumoured, built a base for U-boats in an inlet on the island.) The northern shore formed Nassau's public beach, known as Paradise Beach, and Hunt proposed – sensibly – to rename the island Paradise Island. Would I be interested in taking charge of this project? Well, I said, I thought I ought first to have a look at the place. And on 7 December 1959 I found myself clambering up into the overhead bunk, which was available to a first-class passenger on a Bristol Britannia. We put down briefly at Goose Bay, where it was very cold, and at Idlewild (now Kennedy) where, indoors, it was stiflingly hot. Take-off was alarming: we were buffeted through swirling clouds for what seemed an age, eventually emerging into the sun and heading south.

The Bahamas are not Caribbean, but Atlantic. They have no height and – apart from palms – little natural vegetation;

they are not much more than the tops of coral reefs. But the visual conjunction of sea- and sky-scape can be wonderful. And the climate – seasonal hurricanes apart – is temperately hot, without being exhaustingly humid.

A launch at my constant disposal, I spent two days on and off the island. I swam, not taking too seriously the advice that, if I encountered a shark, I should swim steadily and fiercely towards it and that, if I encountered a barracuda, I should swim like hell away from it. When I could I tested local opinion about Hunt's plans for the island and discovered that by and large – though hardly formulated – they were welcome: tourism was rapidly taking over from fishing and from trade in the natural sponge, which had been killed stone dead by the synthetic kind. As to the island itself, there was more than enough space for an open-air arena, a concert hall and a picture gallery. Wenner-Gren's luxurious home, predictably called Shangri-La, would, I thought, make a useful Festival Club.

Before flying back to New York, I made a point of meeting John and Sylvia Beadle, young English residents in Nassau. John was a wonderfully gifted master of *trompe l'œil* and I once saw a visitor to their tiny home by the sea exclaim, "What a beautiful piece of Wedgwood!" But the piece, and its niche, were illusory. John was employed by the Nassau municipality and, with Sylvia, he had established a small business, the Chelsea Pottery – an oddly inappropriate name, I thought, though by all accounts it flourished.

Another pleasure was the chance of hearing Blake Alphonso Higgs – 'Blind Blake' – the acknowledged master of Bahamian calypso, who sang (and played banjo) at the Royal Victoria Hotel with a small backing group. Blind since his mid-teens, he numbered among his fans the Duke of Windsor, Governor of the Bahamas from 1940 to 1945, about whom he sang 'Love, Love Alone', whose 'ablication' (sic) was the subject of the composition. More stirring, I remember, was

'Run-Come-See Jerusalem' ("Jeroozilem"), which recalled an incident in the hurricane which devastated the Bahamas in 1929. I have a scratchy but wonderfully evocative LP of these songs.

Even more precious is an LP of *A Thurber Carnival*, a revue which, a Thurberholic, I just managed to see in New York in March 1960. Directed by Burgess Meredith, and approved by the author himself, its cast included Tom Ewell, Peggy Cass and Paul Ford – and Kenneth Tynan, in *The New Yorker*, described it as "a tonic anthology of the great man's work [...] and easily the funniest show on Broadway". It began and ended with a 'Word Dance', the cast shuffling round the stage in pairs murmuring to each other till, from time to time, the music stopped, as they did, and one of them uttered a 'Thurberism'. I remember three examples of his demented logic with special pleasure:

"How can I be overdrawn when I have all these cheques left?"
"Well, if I called the wrong number, why did you answer the phone?"
"She said he proposed things on their wedding night her own brother wouldn't have suggested!"

Early in 1960 I cabled Hunt, accepting the offer he had made during discussions in December. The die was cast, but whether the throw was lucky remained to be seen. Undoubtedly glamorous, the job was distinctly far-fetched: in my diary I noted that, "my Anglican, Etonian, Guardsman conscience begins ever so slightly to prick me." But when it emerged that my official base would be in New York I felt rather more respectable.

Because 1960 had been a very strenuous year Hunt had agreed that Mimi and I should sail to New York in comfort. We were 'admitted' on 20 September, as were our two miniature dachshunds, Piglet and Beetle; there were no quarantine requirements and quite soon the dogs were being exercised in Central Park, not far from the flat we had found in the high 50s on New York's East Side. My office was a modest apartment in a hotel west of Broadway and secretarial help was provided by Jennifer Cuany, who had been a mainstay of my Edinburgh office. Jennifer, it was rumoured, had wanted to escape from the attentions of Dudley Moore, one of the four stars of *Beyond the Fringe*. In any case she soon met, and married, Michael Shapiro, a musician, with whom she lived happily ever after. A lovely lady.

But working for Hunt, and 'commuting' from time to time to Nassau, rather soon became frustrating. Though immensely rich he had absolutely no steadiness of vision: he was as likely to take the advice of a bimbo he had met in a nightclub (he was an extravagant womaniser) or the guy in the local liquor store as he was to take mine – or, for that matter, that of Winslow Ames, his experienced fine arts adviser, or Joe Mielziner, his theatre man. So, in due course, I told him that, though he needed me, he did not really want me. But, working out my contractual notice, I found time, with Winslow Ames's professional expertise and the financial support of Sir Harold Christie, one of the big 'Bay Street boys' (and an unusually enlightened patron) to organise an exhibition of the superb Bahamian watercolours of Winslow Homer.

We showed them for three weeks early in March 1962, having set up a portentous body, the International Arts Guild of the Bahamas, independent of Hunt's initiative, to promote the show. Winslow Ames's standing was such that we secured loans from, among other grand museums, the Museum of Fine Arts, Boston, and the Brooklyn Museum. Whether their curators realised that the watercolours would be shown in a big room in Government House without air conditioning and often ablaze with fierce Bahamian sunshine is doubtful. But the show – watercolours, engravings and etchings – was lovely and I enjoyed talking about it to parties of schoolchildren, all – of course – black. When it closed, on 24 March, I was at a loose end. None of the American jobs I had shown interest in had materialised and my resources were running low. We had moved from New York's upper 50s to East 46th Street and I had bought, in a 3rd Avenue print shop called Rockman's, a number of unrecognised English watercolours of quality, selling them on advantageously to Spink's.

But return to England seemed sensible, indeed unavoidable, and I arrived at Southampton early in June, leaving Mimi and our dogs behind. A woman of amazing resourcefulness, she contrived to bring them back to England, via France, and to avoid quarantine requirements by the use of mildly soporific canine drugs, an unnaturally capacious bra and a big, shapeless overcoat.

Meanwhile, I had been job-hunting. Spink's, no doubt impressed by my discovery of a Thomas Girtin and an Edward Lear in New York, offered me a part-time job. Intriguing but absurd was the suggestion, made by a friend in the Intelligence services, that I might consider joining him after undergoing the appropriate clearances. I had never thought that I was likely to make a good spy – my height seemed to suggest otherwise, though it occurred to me that it could perhaps be turned to advantage by a kind of double bluff. Happily, sanity prevailed and the offer of a British Council job in Thailand was more realistic. But I reckoned that if I were to follow work in the Bahamas with a post in Bangkok nobody would ever be likely to take me seriously again. So in the end, in September 1962, I settled for the Independent Television Authority, whose offices were in Knightsbridge. I was called Programme Services Officer and I had responsibility for overseeing the 'cultural' output of the independent television companies, including their religion and music programmes. At least I was a fraction closer to music, though religion seemed to preoccupy me. I organised

67

an international conference on Religion in Broadcasting in a Cambridge college and attended a similar gathering at a conference centre in Kikuyu country near Nairobi. There one day on a quiet evening's walk I chanced upon an enclosure with a signboard announcing 'Primates Research Centre'. My head full of religious matters, it took me a moment or two to interpret the announcement correctly.

But I was treading water, going nowhere, so that when Alexander Gibson, whom I had not seen for three years (since the Toy Symphony of 1960), suggested that I might consider heading the administrative staff of the Scottish National Orchestra, I jumped at the chance, quelling shameful thoughts about the possibility that, after Edinburgh, Glasgow – where the orchestra was based – might prove grimy, inelegant.

Little did I know.

# 11

## Glasgow

Between September 1960, when I finished with the Edinburgh Festival, and March 1964, when I started work in Glasgow, there had been little music in my professional life. But Glasgow was alive with it.

The home of the Scottish National Orchestra and of Scottish Opera, it was also the headquarters of BBC Scotland, whose Symphony Orchestra was increasingly interesting and, under Norman Del Mar, enterprising. The Royal Scottish Academy of Music and Drama, now the Royal Conservatoire of Scotland and the cradle of many good young singers, was presided over by the kindly Henry Havergal, who once gave me some sound advice: when involved in a fierce dispute it was important, he said, to conduct oneself *"suaviter in modo, fortiter in re"* (gently in manner, firmly in deed). At Glasgow University the Music Department was headed by the composer Robin Orr. There was a lot going on. And, music apart, the Citizens' Theatre was on the brink of a memorable phase, better known, I'm sure, in Europe than south of the Border.

Into this civilised milieu, though a Sassenach, I was welcomed in a manner quite beyond Edinburgh's prim reserve. (Occasionally, when severely provoked, I have told an Edinburgh prune that Edinburgh would be the finest city in the world if only it were inhabited by Glaswegians.) The friends surrounding Alexander Gibson made up a loose group not so small as to be cliquey, nor so big as to constitute a fan club. And these people – lawyers, dons, factors, medics and musicians – were regular concertgoers whose loyalty was seriously tested when, in 1962, the acoustically superb St Andrew's Hall was destroyed by fire and the Orchestra's Saturday night concerts were transferred to the so-called 'Glasgow Concert Hall', actually a one-time cinema, distinctly dingy, in an unsalubrious part of Argyle Street.

In every other respect the orchestra which I took over was on a healthily upward curve. It had the support of the Scottish Arts Council (now Creative Scotland) and of many local authorities. My predecessor, Bill Fell, had established an endowment fund and the musicians who, not long ago, had worked on a 'no play, no pay' basis, now had formal contracts which guaranteed them decent terms and conditions, though the salary was, if not derisory, meagre to say the least. I know that one or two of the musicians with wives and children to support had to resort to social security.

Despite low salaries, membership of the Orchestra was pretty stable and it had developed its own characteristic 'sound', luminous and never – even at *fortissimo* levels – strident. This was, of course, Alex Gibson's doing, as were most of its many other achievements, its leader, Sam Bor (at 18 a founder-member, in 1930, of the BBC Symphony Orchestra) playing an invaluable role as mediator between conductor and instrumentalists. Also important to the smooth running of the Orchestra was its manager, Erik Knussen (of that ilk) – uncle of Oliver and brother of Stuart, at one time Principal Double Bass of the LSO. Erik himself was for a while the SNO's tuba, but the job of Orchestra Manager is too demanding to be combined with a playing role even when the instrument is relatively under-used.

The efficiency of the Orchestra's 'infra-structure' made programme-planning that much easier and the SNO's programmes, concocted by Alex and me in a very happy collaboration were, I like to think, imaginative. I'm certainly doubtful if any other British orchestra matched a record which included, in 1965, the centenary of his birth, the seven symphonies of Sibelius, the Schubert Symphonies in the 1964/65 season, the Schumann Symphonies and the three Concertos in 1965/66. Elgar was celebrated with eight works (including *Falstaff*) in 1966/67 and Dvořák with nine in 1967/68. Rachmaninov's then quite rare Fourth Piano Concerto (with John Ogdon) featured with the three Symphonies and the fine *Symphonic Dances* in 1968/69.

Music by living composers, invariably programmed as a matter of policy, was particularly prominent in 1969/70 when Henze and Thea Musgrave both had two works performed. One work each came from Richard Rodney Bennett, Hugh Wood (his *Scenes from Comus*), Martin Dalby and Thomas Wilson, whose *Touchstone* had been given at the Proms of 1967, the year in which the SNO first played overseas.

The tour was a triumph. Superbly organised by Hans Ulrich Schmid, a German agent uniquely civilised and efficient, it opened with two concerts in Vienna's orchestral holy-of-holies, the Grosses Musikvereinsaal, and ended sixteen days and fourteen concerts later in Rotterdam's splendid De Doelen. En route, there were concerts in Salzburg, Munich and Nuremberg. The Orchestra, by now with 60 strings and quadruple woodwind, surpassed itself and Alex Gibson's professional stamina was beyond praise. As to the soloists – Jacqueline du Pré (Schumann, Dvořák and Elgar) and Janet Baker (Mahler's *Kindertotenlieder* and *Rückert-Lieder*) – they were heaven-sent (and, at £100 each per concert, a bargain, even in 1967). There was of course some British music, Britten's powerful (and uncharacteristic) *Sinfonia da Requiem* getting eight performances, his Purcell Variations three, its fugal finale serving as a useful encore. Walton's *Portsmouth Point* Overture got a look in with two. The symphonies were by

71

Brahms (No. 2), Tchaikovsky (No. 4), Sibelius (No. 2) on the whole coolly received, and Prokofiev (No. 5).

For musicians not accustomed to travelling much further afield than Aberdeen, the daily journeys by coach (not conducive to sleep) added to the stresses and strains of unfamiliar beds and food, let alone the challenging necessity of playing to new audiences at the top of their form. But there were some odd bonuses, one of them a welcome erosion of the Them and Us syndrome – the management and the musicians. One day I found myself sitting next to a violinist, Michael Smith, and as we chatted I learned that he was a radio ham, who had recently had an amazing encounter over the airwaves. Twiddling his knobs he had picked up a signal and the following exchange had taken place:

Voice: What is your name?
M.S.: My name is Michael.
Voice: What do you do?
M.S.: I am a violinist in a Scottish orchestra. What is *your* name?
Voice: Hussein.
M.S.: And what do you do?
Voice: I am a king.

It was Hussein of Jordan. And Michael Smith was no longer a featureless fiddler bowing precisely together with thirteen other Second Violins.

The Orchestra returned to Glasgow trailing clouds of journalistic glory. Indeed, press coverage had been so complimentary that with extra help from Scottish Television – which, with the British Council, had been the chief sponsor of the tour itself – we published an illustrated booklet making use of a rough diary I had kept and recording the Orchestra's triumphant progress. Already a national concert asset its status was further enhanced by its contribution to the work of Scottish

Opera, whose first years under Alex Gibson, Robin Orr (chairman) and Peter Hemmings, its remarkable administrator, developed faultlessly. Its programme policy was brave, to say the least: the opening season, in June 1962, had comprised two works, *Madama Butterfly* – an obvious crowd-puller – and *Pelléas et Mélisande*, obviously *not* a popular piece, its subtle half-lights, its *quasi parlando* mode of delivery and its silences seeming to suggest a crowd-deterrent. But business was more than good enough, *Pelléas* attracting 3000, *Butterfly* 5000 customers in a single week of three performances of each opera. And that *Pelléas* was not a flash in Scottish Opera's pan was proved by the inclusion, next year, of the British premiere of Dallapiccola's *Volo di notte* (in a double bill with Ravel's *L'heure espagnole*).

For these works and indeed for every production during my time in Glasgow (which was to end in the autumn of 1972) the SNO was the only orchestra involved. The range of its work was remarkable and it was fortunate to play for *Otello, Boris Godunov, Falstaff* (with Geraint Evans) and *The Trojans*, in which Janet Baker was the intensely moving Dido (and Ronald Dowd her admirable Aeneas). She used to practise in my flat, where I was by then living alone, and to leave me little thank-you notes in one of which she told me that she had "flapped it [the score of *Rosenkavalier*] about under Alex's nose" – and evidently with some effect, for that glorious marshmallow of a comedy came into Scottish Opera's repertoire in the winter of 1970. There were strong echoes of the earlier *Così fan tutte*: producer and designer were again Anthony Besch and John Stoddart; Janet and Elizabeth Harwood, Fiordiligi and Dorabella in *Così*, were now Sophie and Octavian, both stylishly sung. And I mean no slight to Liz Harwood (whose recording of the full version of Zerbinetta's aria in Strauss's *Ariadne auf Naxos* is spectacular) if I concentrate upon Janet's sheer versatility: in *The Trojans* the besotted queen, the noble sufferer; in *Rosenkavalier* the gallant young (male) lover; in *Così* the flighty younger sister. She was at home in them all and in *Così* displayed an unexpected gift for light comedy. In Act 2, at the end of the recitative before the duet in which the sisters choose their 'Albanians' Janet, planting a jaunty feather in her head-dress, declared "I've *quite* decided" ("Io già decisi!"), to captivating effect. (All three operas were sung in English.)

This *Così* had first been heard in 1967, an *annus mirabilissimus* for the Orchestra which, having given Stravinsky's *The Rake's Progress* (under Alex) and Haydn's *Orfeo ed Euridice* (under Richard Bonynge), together with four Stravinsky works, spread over two concerts at the Edinburgh Festival, then split itself into two and visited the Highlands and Islands. I travelled with Raymond Leppard, an entertaining colleague, the uttermost antithesis of the dour Free Church of Scotland representative who greeted us in Stornoway on the Isle of Lewis with the warning that "folks" would not be coming to our "concert" (he spat the word out as if it described a shameless sex-show). Happily, he was quite wrong: the hall was crowded by a warm and receptive audience few, if any, of whom had heard a symphony orchestra before. And the same was true of Kirkwall in the Orkneys, and of Lerwick, even further north in the Shetlands – both visited during the same short tour of the Islands.

Within a month the Orchestra was in Vienna, playing to an audience of the utmost sophistication. And before it was home in Glasgow *The Times* had printed a news item headed "Scottish orchestra proves itself in Vienna", which ended, "A major orchestra – and conductor – would appear to be in the making. The international credentials, in any case, have been earned."

The tour was indeed the highest of high points, but there had been others, the 1965 Edinburgh Festival memorable, at the opening concert, for a Mahler Eighth Symphony with a stellar cast, the female soloists including Heather Harper, Gwyneth Jones and Janet Baker. The following year William Glock, who was not Alex Gibson's warmest admirer, nevertheless invited him to bring his orchestra to the Proms in some more Mahler, this time *Das Lied von der Erde* with – who else? – Janet Baker. As to the tenor, I remember Josef Krips once telling me that the piece really calls for *two* male singers: a *heldentenor* for the first song, a lyric for the others. In the event Richard Lewis spanned the two 'voices' as well as anyone I have ever heard. And Janet, in the last song, I found even more moving, because more subtly expressive, than Kathleen Ferrier. Her Mahler credentials were immaculate, as indeed were Alex's and the Orchestra's.

By now the SNO was broadcasting regularly and beginning to make commercial recordings – with Adrian Boult Elgar's Second Symphony; with Alex a very idiomatic Sibelius disc and a Scottish programme comprising works by Thea Musgrave, Robin Orr and Iain Hamilton. Its many contributions to the Edinburgh Festival were by no means *ex officio* and its regular London visits were either to the Proms or were self-promotions. Twice these visits were combined with concerts at Eton where my brother Nigel Jaques, a beak there, was helpful in making them possible. They were successful, but at the first, in 1968, there was an 'incident'. Towards the end of Elgar's Enigma Variations wisps of smoke began to float out from one of the doorways immediately behind the orchestra and, a second or two later, Erik Knussen appeared with an urgent signal to me (I was sitting near the audience door). The fire had been put out, he said, but "it was deliberate". And so it proved: there was a known arsonist at the school. But – needless to say – "the band played on": Elgar's variations were concluded and Eton's School Hall preserved.

Eton and Glasgow are worlds apart, yet I found that I felt as much at home in the friendly bustle of Scotland's biggest city as in the collegiate cloisters of England's best-known school. But I am grateful to both – and my Glasgow years were exceptionally rich in arts activity. In 1965 I was seconded by the Orchestra so as to take on the directorship of the Commonwealth Arts Festival, one of Ian Hunter's most brilliant of brainchildren, a huge jamboree promoted in London, Cardiff and Glasgow. It was enormous fun: a Great Dance Gala featured drummers and dancers, some on stilts, others low-lying limboists, a steel band and a group quite innocently displaying pretty black breasts. Yehudi Menuhin shared a platform with Ravi Shankar and symphony orchestras from Winnipeg and Sydney brought some Canadian and Australian works. There were exhibitions, films, seminars, a Commonwealth Ceilidh, a Festival Folkboat and a Festival Finale with fireworks. A small spin-off – of which, having originated it, I was proud – was a little book, *Glasgow at a Glance*, a record of Glasgow's best, or at least best-known, buildings, with getting on for 300 photos and a helpful commentary, which was often reprinted. Not among the buildings recorded – because not free-standing – was the City Hall, an unused hall of assembly in Glasgow's Fruit Market. Though small, with a capacity of not much more than 1000, it was of the classic Leipzig, shoe-box, pattern, with warm acoustics and good sight-lines. And there, after four miserable years in Argyle Street, the Orchestra moved in the autumn of 1968. Its first concert programme was apt –

Britten: The National Anthem
Britten: The Building of the House
Mozart: Piano Concerto in B flat, K.450
Mahler: Symphony No. 1

– and the soloist in the Mozart was the great Sviatoslav Richter.

Less elegant, but a lot bigger, was the Kelvin Hall, an all-purpose arena, around the back-stage of which the musicians swore there was more than a whiff of circus-animal, probably elephantine, excretion. Here the Orchestra gave a short summer season of Proms, the atmosphere relaxed but attentive, the Last Night rituals properly Scottish. But the programmes were serious and I recall, in 1966, a very fine Dvořák Concerto from Rostropovich, after which I took him to the station to catch the sleeper to London. It was a Saturday night and Slava was quizzically intrigued by the unbridled conduct of Glasgow youth: "Kissing?" he remarked as he stepped on to the London train.

More important than Glasgow's Proms was the launch in the spring of 1971 of Musica Nova. Conceived by Fred Rimmer, who had succeeded Robin Orr at Glasgow University, and taken up enthusiastically by Alex Gibson, it was a five-day event – more *conversazione* than Festival – four days of public rehearsal and discussion in the University's Bute Hall and a final concert in the City Hall. The composers featured were three Scots – Thea Musgrave, Thomas Wilson and Iain Hamilton – and the international luminary Luciano Berio, whose *Bewegung* (Movement) the composer conducted in Glasgow, as he did at the Edinburgh Festival later the same year in a version somewhat expanded and described as 'definitive'. (Later still *Bewegung* acquired a companion-piece, *Still.*) Tom Wilson had his *Te Deum* performed twice on consecutive nights with Walton's *Belshazzar's Feast* at the Festival, Alex Gibson adding some Stravinsky and, as a finale to the Orchestra's three concerts, Janáček's splendid Sinfonietta.

Of course, not everything was successful. A concert at the Bergen Festival in May 1969 had been sub-standard: everyone

77

had seemed tired. And negotiations for an American tour, which took me to New York, had turned sour. But, all in all, things had gone well, the Orchestra's quality had never been higher and Alex's musicianship and authority had grown to encompass Mozart (*Così*), Berlioz (*The Trojans*), Wagner (*The Ring*) and, among living composers, Berio, Henze and the Scots – Musgrave, Orr and Hamilton. I have referred to his Mahler and I recall with special pleasure Mendelssohn's 'Italian' Symphony.

When the BBC beckoned and I decided to answer its call I left Glasgow with heartfelt regret. The city's generosity was manifested in various ways – among them a formal dinner and, much more enjoyable, a party chez Alex and his adorable wife, Veronica, during which I was persuaded, rather too easily, to play (secondo) with him some of the *Souvenirs de Bayreuth* – snook-cocking duets by Fauré and Messager which send up, with elegant wit, Wagner's pomposities. Leaving this gathering in the small hours and – somehow – finding my way home, I was reminded of a story I had been told as epitomising a particular aspect of Glasgow life: A man leaves his local at closing-time with a half-bottle of whisky in his back pocket. It is raining outside. He slips and falls. Feeling dampness around his hip, he exclaims, "Christ: I hope it's blood!"

Glaswegians – very sensibly – drink a good deal of whisky (the best malts pure nectar) and I joined them in this convivial habit, learning, during eight rewarding years, how – and how not – to drink, whether grape or grain.

Some such spirit must have inspired the Lament which (though, to my shame, I have forgotten who wrote it) recorded my departure from Glasgow:

## A Lament fur Lang Rab

Like Whittington turning to London,
Like Oliver asking for More,
Our Robert's away to the fleshpots
Abandoning Gibson and Bor[1]!

*Refrain:* What have Keller and Boulez and Salter[2]
To offer – we ask and deplore –
That can break up the S.N.O. trio
Of Ponsonby, Gibson and Bor?

What are Barker and Corbett sans Cleese[3]?
What are Alex and Sam without you?
There's a tall empty space at the Proms,
And a void in the Buttery[4] too –

For in Anderton's echoing vaults
We hear, like the boom of a conch,
The ghost of the voice that once cried
"I asked for my spinach EN BRANCHE!"

The Elizabeth wails for its loss,
Kirklee[5] literati despair:
Dame Jean[6] has a nervous prostration
And Maisie[7] is tearing her hair...

---

[1] Sam Bor, the Orchestra's leader
[2] Hans Keller, Pierre Boulez and Lionel Salter, future BBC colleagues
[3] The Two Ronnies (Barker and Corbett) and John Cleese
[4] A restaurant where, apparently, I insisted
[5] I lived in Kirklee Circus
[6] Dame Jean Roberts, a past Lord Provost (sic) of Glasgow and Vice-Chairman of the Orchestra's Board. Seemingly fierce and formidable, she was actually kindly and humorous
[7] Maysie Connell, one of two hospitable, well-upholstered, spinster-sisters, devoted supporters of the Orchestra

79

For our Robert's away ower the Border
To the glamour and glare of TV,
And Radio Three is the richer
For R.P. H.Mus. B.B.C.

But wherever your talents may find you,
Dear Robert, although you fare forth,
let a sniff at the snuff-box[8] remind you
Of friends you have left in the North!

*Refrain:* What have Keller and Boulez and Salter
To offer – we ask and deplore –
That can break up the S.N.O. trio
Of Ponsonby, Gibson and Bor?

---

[8] A pretty Scottish 18th-century snuff-box – one of several leaving presents

# 12

## Cumbria 1 – Cragg Cottage

This chapter, about my Cumbrian roots, was circulated to family and friends in 1995.

In April 1969 I bought a tiny cottage in the village of Buttermere in the Lake District. I had been visiting the Buttermere valley since about 1943, when Claude Elliott, Headmaster (and later Provost) of Eton, had proposed a holiday there. It was a family affair and we stayed at what is now the Youth Hostel. Claude had a house, Lower Gatesgarth, further up the valley. After breakfast we would foregather there and he would lead us on day-long walks in the surrounding hills. These he knew like the back of his hand.

The Buttermere scenery is magnificent. The valley runs NW/SE and it encompasses two lakes – Buttermere to the south, Crummock Water to the north – with a linking stream, the Dubbs, of crystal clarity, on which a pair of dippers can often be seen. Buttermere village – a church, an erstwhile school, three farms, two hotels, a youth hostel and seven houses – lies between them. The encircling peaks – Grassmoor, Whiteless Pike, Robinson, Hinds Garth, Dale Head to the east; Fleetwith and Haystacks to the south; High Crag, High Stile and Red Pike to the west – are extremely steep, rising from about 300 feet to the highest at more than 2500 feet. These steep gradients have the advantage that – unlike the Cairngorms or the Welsh mountains – the Lakeland hills can be climbed very quickly and a good many summits of between 2000 and

3000 feet can be achieved in a single day. During those early years Great Gable was a doddle, we generally managed Scafell and Scafell Pike, sometimes we 'did' the Four Pass walk – over Scarth Gap into Ennerdale (where the most romantic youth hostel in the world is sited), over Black Sail into Wasdale, over Stye Head into Borrowdale and back over Honister into Buttermere.

I fell deeply in love with the place and with the landscape. I also felt, or thought I felt, a sense that I was rediscovering my roots, for Captain John Ponsonby (1634–1703) was my antecedent and he had lived at Haile Hall, over the hills to the west. Nearby, within sight of Sellafield, are the village of Ponsonby, Ponsonby Church and Ponsonby Old Hall. And in the telephone book there is a handful of other Ponsonbys.

So the purchase of Cragg Cottage was some kind of a return to ancestral roots as well as the acquisition of a bolt-hole in which relaxation and refreshment were instantly available. It was twenty years before I installed a telephone, but a shower was an immediate need (there was no bathroom, though a loo) and in the larder, across the end of which there was a superb slate, waist-high, on which hams had once been cured, the ideal space could be created. In the kitchen I installed a small solid-fuel Rayburn. And that was about all that then needed to be done. There were two bedrooms, a living-room and a porch on the garden side. The garden itself was eccentrically shaped, dull and unsecluded. So I planted shrubs – berberis, weigela, viburnum and buddleia – to protect me from the road, beech and cotoneaster hedges to screen me from my neighbours. I raised the upper part of the garden to form a rough patio, planting herbs and helianthemum between the paving-stones. Around the tiny lawn I grew wild roses, ramblers and – much later – a splendid Blanc Double de Coubert; and, on the side of the house, a climbing hydrangea. Lower down I put in azaleas and some small rhododendrons. I say "I", but I had the help of

Lesley Black, whom I was to marry in 1977. At one time a student at the Royal Scottish Academy of Music and Drama, Lesley was a very good flautist and a woman of the utmost practical good sense. Disconcertingly observant, she taught me – or tried to teach me – many of the Scottish virtues. She could be unhesitatingly direct and this was good for me: I tended to be mealy-mouthed when dealing with awkward human predicaments. In the garden we made a good complementary pair, I the strategist, she the tactician. By which I suppose I mean that she was better than me at the drudgery of weeding. In any case, we were very happy at Cragg Cottage and before our relationship ended in 1985 she challenged me to risk doing Jack's Rake, a steep, very exposed scramble on Pavey Ark. We did it together. She herself had earlier pioneered a precipitous route up Red Pike. One day we found a tiny ash seedling barely six inches high and we transplanted it to a more strategic point where, at over twenty feet, it now offers dappled shade to the paved part of the garden. And shade – notwithstanding Cumbria's reputation for rain – is often needed in May and June, months when around Rannerdale the fields are a carpet of bluebells and the hedges are full of wild roses.

I have been to Buttermere at every season and in all weathers. I remember a drive from Glasgow, in dead of winter, and arrival after midnight in an aching pitch-dark frost. One Christmas, Roger Toulmin and I crunched our way through thick snow onto Green Gable, where strong winds made horizontal icicles on the fences. One New Year Lesley and I were snowbound – to our delight – because the snowplough forgot to grit the road to Cockermouth, creating an impassable iced switchback. Often, on a winter night during a bedtime stroll, I have seen my own shadow sharply etched on the road by a full moon. Such nights are still, but the valley endures tremendous winds. They roar down from the north with deafening ferocity. More than once I have watched opposing gusts driving the surface of one of the lakes towards a central collision, where a waterspout has spiralled into the air. Some of these gusts are freakish. One such neatly snapped off, at its base, a pretty camellia in a sheltered corner of my garden. Another – of unimaginable force – lifted off the entire slate roof of a huge nineteenth-century barn at Gatesgarth, near the foot of Fleetwith, and dumped it nearby. Neither the adjacent farm, nor any tree, was even slightly damaged.

And, of course, it rains; by God it rains! A few years ago Cragg Cottage – perhaps because of a shift in the flow of water from the hill, perhaps because of an undetected weakness in its foundations – sprang a leak and during a torrential evening I spent four hours staunching a steady flow of water across the slates which form the floor of the sitting-room. But rain, of course, fills the waterfalls and, when the wind drops, the sound of Sour Milk Ghyll tumbling a thousand feet into the Dubbs across the valley is a comfortable hubbub, over which cattle, sheep and birds provide their solo obbligatos. Sometimes, in windless, dry weather, when the waterfalls are low and the animals and birds are asleep, there is almost literally nothing to be heard – a rare and awing experience (and one which frightened a Scottish friend who – shame on her! – cut short her holiday and returned to the familiar clank and rattle of Glasgow).

To arrive in Buttermere is to rejoin a village community of which, though by local standards still an 'off-comer', I feel a part. We have common concerns about the tiny church (where the amazing Wainwright is remembered in a plaque below a window with a view to Haystacks, his favourite mountain), the village hall (once the school), the state of the roads, the problem of cars (and car parking), the activities of the National Trust, which has much property in the area and is not always sensitive about small local issues. Over the years 'we', the villagers, have often lost to 'them' – anonymous authorities of various kinds. We had a superb water supply, straight off the hill, fresh, natural and delicious. Chlorination was proposed; we objected; the supply was chlorinated. Bureaucrats in Brussels decreed that the rich milk supplied by Syke Farm be designated 'raw, unpasteurised' – and the farmer lost his orders from the Bridge and Fish Hotels. The National Trust sought our advice about the siting of a new car park. We voted for a central location; the Trust decreed a peripheral one. Most sensationally, the County Council, in an attempt to avoid the occasional traffic jam (generally caused by two monstrous coaches proceeding in opposite directions) proposed to mark the roads around and through the village with double yellow lines. (The National Trust feebly suggested thin green ones.) The village objected and, on the late December day when the heavy mechanical vehicles arrived, sat down in the road in great numbers. But in the background were policemen with a Black Maria and, after the failure of negotiation, the vicar and his wife, the chairman of the Parish Council and his, together with several other protesters, were taken away to Workington and charged with obstruction. A shameful affair for, of course, what we had forecast turned out to be true – that the lines were urban, unsuitable and unsightly; that they could not be monitored, and that, if observed, they would only move the potential traffic jam to another part of the valley.

It is a fact that Buttermere, like many Lakeland valleys, endures too many coaches, too many cars and too many sedentary trippers. But the hills cannot ultimately be spoiled and the enterprising walker can get away from the crowds without difficulty. Even easily accessible beauty spots such as the foreshore of Crummock Water are often deserted if one visits them early or late. This small stroll, through Long How Wood, is one I nowadays undertake almost every day when I am at Cragg Cottage. In spring and early summer one can generally see pied flycatchers, redstarts, treecreepers, willow

85

and wood warblers, blue, great and long-tailed tits and great spotted woodpeckers. On the beck there are often dippers. (Lesley and I, in a hard winter, once heard them singing: a low warbling sound.) On Crummock Water itself there are resident sandpipers, heron and cormorants. Duck regularly include goldeneye. Great crested grebe are common, merganser recurrent. Of geese, Canadas and greylags are also common, but I have seen a single snow-goose and a single barnacle. On a still morning the reflection of Melbreak can be magical.

One February day I walked around Buttermere in warm sunshine while two separate layers of horizontal mist hung in the air: one carpeted the surface of the lake and another obscured the waistline of the mountains so that their lower slopes and their summits were visible, their midriffs obscured.

Cragg Cottage sits in an enclave of five cottages, three of them permanently occupied, and my good neighbours keep an eye on it. It has never been let, but friends and relations stay there and without exception they have found it friendly, peaceful and relaxing. I have no TV set and only a transistor radio – and that mainly for the weather forecast. I like to think that the total change of lifestyle, climate and environment, the wholly different aural background (including the absence of music), the slower pace of country life and a circle of warm-heartedly Cumbrian friends have contributed to my well-being, conceivably to my (at present) modest longevity.

Whatever the case, I have loved Buttermere valley for fifty years and Cragg Cottage for more than twenty-five. I bought it with a small legacy from my grandmother, Mary Ponsonby – a gifted painter in watercolour – upon whom blessings!

# Gallery

*1927, Oxford. Mother, son and period pram*

*1931, Ely. At the grave of a pet dog*

*1937, Prep School. On stage as poker-bending Dr Grimesby Rylott in 'The Speckled Band'*

*1946. Second Lieutenant, Scots Guards*
*(Photo: Hay Wrightson)*

*1956, Edinburgh. Meeting Prince Philip in the Assembly Hall at a performance of 'Henry V' by Stratford Ontario Festival Company (Photo: Paul Shillabeer)*

*1960 (10 September). Toy Symphony with, in foreground, Mstislav Rostropovich (back of head), Gennadi Rozhdestvensky, Leonide Massine, Alexander Gibson and members of the RPO (Photo: The Scottish Tourist Board)*

*1961, Jacksonville, Florida. Delius's Solano Grove home, restored and resited on University campus, photographed en route, by car, from New York to Miami (Photo: the author)*

*1974. With Pierre Boulez at a pre-Prom talk*

*1981, London. 'Music of Eight Decades' press conference. William Glock, John Casken, Peter Maxwell Davies, RP, Nigel Osborne, Simon Rattle (Photo: Keystone Press Agency)*

*1981 (10 September). With Daniel Barenboim and Margaret Thatcher awaiting President Mitterand for a Prom by the Orchestre de Paris (Photo: BBC)*

*1983. Ronald Dickinson's pastel portrait of Lesley, the author's wife*

*In Cumbria, with Bitter*

*1984, USA. Joe Coolidge with Grace*

*1992, Barcelona. The lone guitarist in the Plaça del Rei*

*1996. In Orkney for Peter Maxwell Davies's Sixth Symphony
(Photo: Judy Arnold)*

# 13

## An Honourable Trio

On 25 July 1975 – the day on which the Proms season opened – I was made an Honorary Member of the Royal Academy of Music and asked to reply on behalf of Malcolm Arnold and Robert Donington, also made Honorary Members. This is what I said:

Mr Chairman, Principal, ladies and gentlemen, it is a matter of great pride to me that you have asked me to reply on behalf of Malcolm Arnold and Robert Donington, and I do so with great pleasure and considerable trepidation. Considering what I should say on this occasion, it struck me that the BBC's policy – which is to inform, educate and entertain – was perhaps reflected in the three of us.

Malcolm Arnold was referred to only last week as a composer of entertainment music, whatever that may mean; Mr Donington, through his scholarship and his musicology, has been a very great educator of musical taste; and I like to think that in my position I am able to inform music-lovers through the various channels of the BBC. But, reflecting on this, I came to the conclusion that this was really altogether too crude. Mr Arnold's prowess as a trumpet player has already been referred to, and in fact he played for Sir Henry Wood on one or two occasions. He is also a fine conductor. As a composer I think that he would feel, and I would share this view, that he would prefer to be known by that part of his music which is less entertaining than that which is best known.

As for Mr Donington, he is of course much more than merely a scholar and musicologist; he is a gifted and celebrated performer, as has been said, on the viola da gamba and on the violin. He is also a broadcaster of distinction, and this is in itself an art.

For my own part I am quite happy to be regarded as an administrator in music, although I did once appear under Mr Arnold's baton and actually got the part right, whereas Sir Jack Westrup, who was sharing it with me, failed to do so. I also feel that through the BBC I can participate not only in information but in education and in entertainment.

However you may like to regard us, I would like to say that we receive these honours with the greatest pleasure, and with pride. I would also like to add that I am delighted that this honour should come my way on the day of the opening of the Proms and at about the time of publication of a book about your first Principal, Doctor William Crotch, who was a very civilised man (although perhaps not a very great composer) and somebody in whom I have long been interested, not for his musical qualifications but because he was an extremely good painter in water-colours.

Now I have been asked to say a word or two to the graduates here today, about their future in the profession, and although I do not think I am very well qualified to do so, I will try, because I have known a large number of musicians. The first thing I want to say is very boring, and that is that all the really important and successful musicians that I have known have worked extremely hard, from morning to night throughout their lives. Sir Henry Wood, it is often forgotten, conducted every one of the Proms in the early years, and there was a Prom more or less every day and the season lasted for eight to ten weeks, and he did this on one rehearsal, and I don't quite know how, but he managed. Sir Thomas Beecham, who liked to be thought of as something of a dilettante, in fact prepared his scores extremely carefully. I once came upon him in an Edinburgh hotel bowing the parts of Beethoven's 'Choral' Symphony, and he was rather upset to have been discovered so doing, and passed off this discovery with the remark, "I have been composing the symphonies of Beethoven." M Pierre Boulez, with whom I am closely associated, conducts not only the BBC Symphony Orchestra but the New York Philharmonic, and directs a research centre in acoustic and musical techniques in Paris, and I can say without question that none of these three enormously responsible posts is undertaken with anything but the most rigorous energy. And, if Mrs Vaughan Williams will forgive me, because this reference is made with affection, a friend of mine once visited Ralph Vaughan Williams for breakfast, and at the end of the meal Vaughan Williams, upon whose forelock a small morsel of toast remained, pushed back his chair and said, "Well, I suppose I had better go and do some compo"; in other words, it was a daily routine and a discipline.

Now if you are going to be a composer, I hope that you will follow Malcolm Arnold's practice and be true to your own stylistic inclination. Don't join the *avant garde* because it is fashionable to do so, but don't on the other hand close your ears to what the *avant garde* is doing, because that *may* be the way ahead – only recall what happened at the first performance of Stravinsky's *Rite of Spring*.

If you are going to be a solo performer you must have an immaculate technique, but that is really only the beginning, because your technique is no more than a servant to your own interpretative ideas, and these ideas will only flow from you if you have lived and thought about life, and have travelled if not in body, then in mind. Janet Baker, whom you all know, whenever she travels has what she calls a book-bag – a bag full of books, and the books are not novelettes but books of philosophy and history and archaeology and books about the arts, and that is why she is such a very great interpreter of music: because she brings to bear upon her performances a wealth of knowledge of other subjects on important other matters.

I hope none of you will despise the orchestral profession. There was a time when the orchestral musician was a somewhat down-trodden member of society. That has all changed. He is now – he or she – well regarded, reasonably well paid, and, particularly outside London, lives and works in civilised and well-organised situations. The security of the orchestral life is much greater than it used to be, again possibly excepting the London orchestras, and the standards of all our orchestral playing are now extremely high.

I know that in this building you won't despise teaching. We need more teachers and better teachers; we need more milk in order to have more cream in the profession. And, finally, I hope you won't forget that scholarship in itself, and broadcasting as an immense educative force, are careers well worthy of following. So, whether you turn out to be a composer who conducts, or a scholar who performs, or an administrator who is involved in music at every level, I wish you extremely well, I wish you every success, and every happiness in your musical careers.

# 14

## BBC Days and Nights

When I joined the BBC on 1 December 1972 I was succeeding the formidable William Glock as Controller, Music – a post surely more accurately designated Controller, Classical Music, Radio. I had of course consulted William, who had been generous with his advice. I particularly liked his characteristically dissident, "Do it first. Tell them [i.e. the bosses] afterwards." William often did it first and I caught a whiff of this tendency during one of my interviews when it became clear to me that "they" thought he had attached too much importance to the public concert, too little to administration, to studio broadcasting and the art of radio. I remember – to my shame – a glib remark I made to the effect that whereas William was a musician in administration, I thought of myself as an administrator in music. I have reason to believe that this went down well – and in due course my appointment was confirmed.

It was very odd. Though I was a practised administrator, I had no broadcasting experience at all: my short spell with the ITA had been pure bureaucracy. And if I had any particular strength it was in the planning of public concerts. Moreover I had always told myself that I would never work for a really big organisation. But, like Alexander Goehr in the 1960s, I found the offer irresistible, Sandy's capitulation necessitated by financial need, mine justified, I suppose, by the possibility of influence.

In Glasgow my administrative staff had numbered less than a dozen; at the BBC I would have responsibility for more than a hundred. And among those colleagues were such luminaries as Deryck Cooke, Lionel Salter, Julian Budden, Robert Simpson, Robert Layton and Hans Keller – all of them experts in their particular fields, all of them fascinating personalities, not all of them very easy human beings. (I remember Howard Newby, in another guise the fine novelist P.H. Newby, who was then Director of Programmes in BBC Radio – and so my boss – advising me to be sensitive in my dealings with Simpson, because of a past illness, and Keller, because of his hair-raisingly narrow escape from the Nazis in 1938.)

So I had a good many Munros to climb – and not much time to climb them: there were pressing issues to be dealt with, the most pressing, and the most public, the appointment of a successor to Pierre Boulez as Chief Conductor of the BBC Symphony Orchestra. Pierre's contract had less than two years to run, which, in the diary of an eminent musician, is not much more than the twinkling of an eye. I had given the question a lot of thought and, because a broadcasting orchestra needs a very much bigger repertoire than a 'public' orchestra, it had seemed to me that some kind of a triumvirate was called for, one of the three self-evidently the 'Chief'. So I came up with Georg Solti, Colin Davis and Pierre, who had offered me occasional guest visits. Georg, I believed, would bring to the Orchestra a glamour which I thought it would welcome, and some recordings, of which it had not recently made many. I saw him early in 1973 and he told me that before he could reach a decision he must conduct the Orchestra at a public concert. Luckily I was able to find him a Prom on 23 July 1973, when György Pauk (also Hungarian) was the soloist in Mozart's Violin Concerto No. 4 in D and Georg himself gave us a powerful Bruckner 7. The concert was a success and I began to be hopeful, but a last hurdle had to be cleared. It concerned contractual and personnel matters and it called for dealings with top administrative brass. So Ian Trethowan, Radio's Managing Director, and I flew to Paris in early September when Georg quizzed us in great detail about the personnel, the rehearsals, the contract, studio recording conditions, public concerts (including particularly the Proms) and the possibility of commercial recordings.

In the end – and fairly soon – Georg turned us down and my master-plan collapsed, Colin Davis, always sympathetic and helpful, eventually explaining that his diary was already too full. How very welcome he would have been, particularly in Berlioz and Tippett. Meanwhile I had approached Rudolf Kempe, Georg Solti's successor at the Bavarian State Opera, whom, after strenuous negotiations with his agent, Howard Hartog (who drove a hard bargain), I appointed. Very welcome to the Orchestra, he knew how to address them, having himself once been principal oboe in the Leipzig Gewandhaus Orchestra. But, unhappily, his reign lasted barely a year; he died in Zurich on 12 May 1976, his widow, Cordula, a violinist, settling in Stratford-upon-Avon and launching a regular series of recitals combining chamber music and verse, with actors from the Royal Shakespeare Company.

Kempe's early death left me with a problem: he had himself been a Plan B. I considered the possibilities and, having consulted Lilian Hochhauser, who knew more than anyone about Soviet cultural relations, decided to approach Gennadi Rozhdestvensky, a Soviet citizen. "You never know," said Lilian; "I should have a go. He might very well want the job."

Gennadi had been my co-triangulist (with Rostropovich) in the Toy Symphony at Edinburgh in 1960. So we were acquainted. But I was a BBC man and the Soviet authorities much disliked what they heard on the BBC external channels about the Soviet Union. And Gennadi (whom I caught at

107

London Airport early in 1977) confirmed that, though he was indeed very interested, the negotiations – if not abortive – would be laboriously slow, such was the nature of Soviet bureaucracy. I was in two minds, but his self-evident interest in, and amazingly extensive knowledge of, English music decided me and I embarked upon negotiations. These – to my surprise – went quite quickly and after about eight months I went to Moscow with a colleague, Bill Relton, manager of the Orchestra, linguist and genial companion, the absolute antithesis of the cold, po-faced bureaucrats we encountered. We were told that Gennadi's appointment was approved and we cabled him in Stockholm, agreeing a press conference in London on 1 November. This went well: his idiosyncratic conducting style and his charm achieved a *Times* leader and the appointment of a Soviet citizen to a BBC orchestra was greeted with warm, if surprised, approval.

The first concert I could find for Gennadi was a Prom on 9 September 1978, more than two years since his predecessor's last concert. During this hiatus I had endured some caustic teasing from *Private Eye*. But the concert obliterated all such memories. The programme was obviously apt –

Mozart: Symphony No. 32 in G
Britten: Diversions for piano (left hand) and orchestra
Shostakovich: Symphony No. 4 in C minor

The soloist in the Britten was Gennadi's wife, Victoria Postnikova, who had shared second prize at the Leeds Piano Competition in 1966, when many thought she had deserved to win. The work, which she played with panache, was welcome, because rarely performed. (Gennadi was heard to remark at the time, "Why, if you have two hands, do you not use them both?") The symphony was, of course, powerfully idiomatic.

So the Symphony Orchestra had a Chief Conductor and at about the same time I appointed Michael Gielen as a Chief Guest, joining Charles Mackerras in this dual role. Michael's repertoire in part replaced Boulez's: he had conducted British premieres of Messiaen and Schoenberg on earlier visits to the Orchestra and he was a champion of Zemlinsky and Zimmermann. During the 1980 Proms he premiered Alexander Goehr's *Babylon the Great is Fallen*, a big choral work marking the fiftieth birthday of the BBC Symphony Chorus. He was an admirable musician handicapped only by a speaking voice of grating harshness. But he did us proud, his swan-song a memorable *Gurrelieder* (Schoenberg), with Jessye Norman and John Tomlinson among the cast, during the 1981 Proms.

Meanwhile, Gennadi was surpassing my hopes for his commitment to English music. During 1980 alone he gave us Alwyn's Fifth Symphony, Tippett's Second and *A Child of Our Time*, Vaughan Williams's Fifth, Delius's *Song of the High Hills* and the Violin Concerto. The musicians' strike (to which I will return) deprived him of Elgar's *The Apostles* and Robin Holloway's *Scenes from Schumann*. His record during 1981 was as remarkable, including, as it did, Britten's *War Requiem* in the Albert Hall and John Tavener's *Akhmatova Requiem* at the Edinburgh Festival.

Then small things began to go wrong. One day, at about 9 a.m., he phoned my Maida Vale Studio staff to say that he was unwell; he could not rehearse at 10 a.m. Desperate efforts were made to reach the 90-odd musicians before they left home – but in many cases unavailingly. Now it happened that day that I was lunching near Hyde Park Corner and because I was early and the weather fine I walked the last quarter-mile or so. Imagine my astonishment when I encountered Gennadi in a dapper cap and carrying a small parcel or two. When he saw me he embarked upon a seriously over-acted charade: he was "terribly ill", he was on his way to the doctor's. Not long afterwards, on a European tour, he cancelled the much-needed rehearsal of a difficult Tippett work before an important concert in Holland. The climax of my dissatisfaction came in 1982 when he was to open the Proms with Berlioz's *The Trojans*. It was a big undertaking and I had allowed enough rehearsal time, so I was alarmed when the agent of Jessye Norman, our Dido, phoned to say that Gennadi had held no piano rehearsals and Jessye was seriously bothered. I could not afford to lose her and, in a quiet talk, I explained to Gennadi that piano rehearsals with the principals were essential – especially as (and I didn't say this) some of his tempi were very unusual. He appeared to acquiesce, but next morning a message reached me via Bill Relton: Gennadi would not conduct the Orchestra as long as I was around. It was hard to know how seriously to take this threat, but I thought it best to lie low, particularly as, apart from *The Trojans*, the first performance of Hugh Wood's big Symphony was due a few days later. In the event, Gennadi delivered a patchy *Trojans*, but a performance of Hugh's Symphony which delighted the composer.

Gennadi's occasional unprofessionalism apart, he was giving us admirable repertoire and was popular with the public and with most of the Orchestra, so an extension of his contract was obviously desirable. I phoned Moscow and arranged a meeting at the Ministry of Culture, having explained my errand. But when I arrived in Moscow with Bill Relton, we found that everything possible went adrift and I later concluded that we had been the victims of a well-planned programme of obstruction and frustration. Nobody met us at the airport, but after a while a scruffy young man, who seemed to know who we were, turned up with a rather battered limousine. Having explained that we had no reservations he took us to a big hotel where, nevertheless, rooms were found. Next day I phoned the Ministry for an appointment, but apparently no meeting had been arranged. We eventually saw the appropriate officials the following morning (the day of our departure), only to be told that no decision could be reached for several months – a message which could very easily have been conveyed by letter or phone. Bill and I went to the airport in disgust and there a final small mortification occurred at the passport desk: a pimply youth took my passport, looked at my photo, looked at me, repeated the action – then disappeared into a back office for five minutes, eventually returning with a more senior colleague who waved me through. But during those five minutes I got a chilling glimpse of the awful predicament of a refugee without the validation which a passport provides.

Gennadi's work with the Orchestra petered out, though he occasionally appeared as a guest, and he continued to propagate English music – and not only in England – to the extent that, years later, in February 2014, he was awarded the CBE by the British Ambassador in Moscow.

Of his successor as the Orchestra's Chief Conductor I had written in a paper dated 24 June 1981 to the BBC's Board of Management that John Pritchard "is a musicians' musician: many regard him as the most gifted British conductor of his generation. The Orchestra, in an informal poll conducted before they knew of his appointment, placed him second only to Haitink as their favoured Chief Conductor. He has immense experience – including much in contemporary music: he introduced Musica Viva to Britain. He was Chief Conductor of the LPO and Musical Director at Glyndebourne. He now works principally in Cologne and Brussels: so he is handy... And he is British: a political plus."

Both Gennadi and John had connections with the musicians' strike of 1980 when the first twenty Proms had to be cancelled. Gennadi was deprived of Elgar's *The Apostles* (at the opening concert), Schnittke's *St Florian Symphony*, Bruckner's Psalm 150, Robin Holloway's *Scenes from*

111

*Schumann* (following Shostakovich's edition of Schumann's Cello Concerto), Stravinsky's *Renard* and *Rag-Time*. A long way from Elgar and Bruckner was Shostakovich's arrangement of Vincent Youmans's 'Tea for Two', or *Tahiti Trot*, the last work lost before the strike ended.

When the Proms resumed on 7 August it was John (with Jessye Norman in Messiaen's *Poèmes pour Mi*) who picked up the pieces. Genial and unflappable, he was ideally cast for an occasion which might have been marred by an 'incident'. I had better explain.

The BBC had decided that it needed to dispose of five ensembles – three Radio Orchestras, the London Studio Players and the Northern Ireland Orchestra. The Radio Orchestras were neither Symphony Orchestras nor Big Bands and distinctly out of date, the Studio Players were good but their role was ill-defined, the Northern Ireland Orchestra was so small as hardly to deserve its title. As Controller, Music, I had no responsibility for the Radio 'orchestras' or for the Studio Players and only a collateral concern for the Northern Ireland Orchestra. So I was not opposed to what was planned, particularly as the real symphony orchestras, of which there were four (in London, Manchester, Glasgow and Cardiff), were to be strengthened. It was the execution of the plan that appalled me and my colleagues.

Negotiations with the Musicians Union were in the hands of Aubrey Singer, who had recently taken over as Managing Director, Radio. Essentially a TV man, Aubrey had brought with him a reputation as a toady to his superiors, a tyrant towards his juniors. He found his transition to Radio difficult to adapt to: for a long time he referred to Radio 3's audience as "viewers". Moreover he had preconceived ideas about me and my staff, apparently regarding us as "musicologists" concerned to broadcast only to other musicologists. This was, of course, rubbish, but it became an *idée fixe* and a convenient stick to beat us with. Unfortunately he adopted the same tone of voice with the Musicians Union when it called its membership out on strike. He boasted that the BBC could, by the use of recordings, sustain the stoppage indefinitely. He clearly believed that, by huffing and puffing, he could blow down the Union's house. The Union, strongly – and subtly – led by John Morton, soon produced a lapel badge with one word on it: Saxinga. Meanwhile, distinguished musicians, friends of mine, among them Charles Groves, Evelyn Rothwell and Geraint Evans 'demonstrated' outside Broadcasting House and BBC musicians played on the steps of All Souls, Langham Place. One day I met the BBC's Head of Personnel, Michael Bett, in the hallway of Broadcasting House and he stopped me: "Robert, I've seen all kinds of strikes, but never one like this one. Those guys playing outside are so *nice*." "Of course," I said, "they are musicians." A friendly phone call came from Colin Davis, who clearly understood the extremely uncomfortable position I found myself in, agreeing the BBC's strategy, but deploring Singer's blustering tactics. "Colin," I said, "do you think I should resign?" "No," said Colin; "I shall always remember what William Glock said to me – 'Never resign: there is no strength in absence.'" (Years later I sought William's advice about another dilemma and he said, "Edward Dent once told me, 'Never resign: there is no strength in absence.'")

So I did not resign and in due course the strike was settled – but not before BBC Scotland, to my utter consternation, decided that it would disband not its Radio Orchestra, but its Symphony Orchestra, thus making nonsense of our central strategy. Working late one evening I had a call from Michael Swann, Chairman of the Board of Governors, who asked me, "What are we going to do about Scotland, Robert?" "You *must* tell them," I said, "that they can't scrap their Symphony Orchestra." "I don't think we can do that," said Swann; "we've only just given them the autonomy which entitles them to." But in the end Scotland's Symphony Orchestra was saved and the strike abandoned thanks to the negotiating skills of Arnold Goodman. The cost to the BBC, however, was considerable: members of the three Radio Orchestras were guaranteed 66 per cent of their annual salaries for five years, while the Northern Ireland Orchestra was in due course amalgamated with the Ulster Orchestra, thus establishing a body of realistic size, to which the BBC contributed a large sum annually.

On the plus side: money was found substantially to increase the number of strings in the Symphony Orchestra and the Northern Symphony Orchestra, which soon renamed itself Philharmonic, thus declaring Manchester's open rivalry with London. Unquestionably, the quality of all four Symphony Orchestras rose steadily in the years following the strike and the BBC's debt to Arnold Goodman was incalculable, the man himself charmingly dauntless. Once, outvoted into a minority of one, he had declared, "Well, gentlemen, we have an impasse." And encountering him after the death of Adrian Boult and remarking that, characteristically, Boult had left his body for medical research, I was captivated by his response: "I shouldn't have thought old Adrian's organs would be much use to anybody."

* * * * *

The strike over and the Proms resumed, I licked my wounds. Aubrey, with typical bully-boy intemperance, had threatened me with the sack and charged me with disloyalty. Even among my immediate colleagues, all of them supportive, I had problems, the most awkward being their vehement wish to write a letter to *The Times* condemning BBC tactics. Sharing their feelings, I had nevertheless to bang the table and to insist that they must first exhaust internal procedures. They could not otherwise bite the hand that was feeding them – the BBC's.

My remaining BBC years were relatively untroubled, though the recent appointment of Ian McIntyre as Controller, Radio 3, caused many of my immediate colleagues – and me – some discomfort. Ian, an experienced radio man and a good broadcaster (later the biographer of John Reith, the BBC's first Director-General) had risen to be Controller, Radio 4, where his abrasive management style went down very badly with his staff and he had to be moved. By what logic the Board of Governors concluded that the Controllership of Radio 3 was just the place for him it is impossible to comprehend. Inevitably we fought and Humphrey Carpenter's report that at a meeting of producers – members of my own staff – Ian told me to "bugger off" is true. It was deplorable and only diminished Ian.

But the administrative structure supporting Radio 3 was dotty. There were two Controllers – Ian of "Radio 3", I of "Music", i.e. of Music Division, whose producers made programmes for, and offered them to, Radio 3. But Ian (like his predecessor, Stephen Hearst) was no musician, was not even 'musical', so that, editorially, he was out of his depth. He nevertheless took a jaundiced view of music producers, regarding them as incestuously inward-looking: a hopeless state of affairs. It was all too obvious that Controller, Radio 3, needed, at the very least, some knowledge of music and, preferably, some qualification in the practice of it. At what point I urged Ian Trethowan to ensure that the next Controller, Radio 3, had music in his background I don't now remember. but the point was taken and in due course John Drummond was appointed, music producers working directly to him and the post of Controller, Music, being subsumed into that of Controller, Radio 3. Some of this reorganisation was being developed – rather uncomfortably for me – during my last year with the BBC, but the transitional arrangements left me free to concentrate upon the work of the Symphony Orchestra, on the Proms and on the live concerts of the European Broadcasting Union.

For seven years I had been the EBU's "Co-ordinator of radio music planning and operations", a citation distinctly over-generous. In fact I chaired regular meetings of music experts from Western European broadcasters and from the USA. (Eastern Europe had its own, similar body.) Sometimes we met in the EBU's elegant, modern headquarters in Geneva; more often we were the guests of this or that broadcaster. I recall, with great pleasure, meetings in Venice, where RAI's 'Broadcasting House' was a palazzo with murals by Tiepolo, a more decorative artist than the BBC's Eric Gill, and in Sveti Stefan, an islet on the Adriatic coast north of Dubrovnik whose inhabitants, we learned, had been turfed out of their very pretty homes by the Belgrade government and rehoused in a jerry-built estate on the mainland, so making way for an elegant conference centre.

The live international concerts which our meetings co-ordinated were hair-raisingly complex. The originating broadcaster – let's say Yugoslavia – provided details of the programme and presentation material in the vernacular, in this case Serbo-Croat. This was forwarded to Brussels, where Belgian Radio circulated it to anything between twelve and twenty other national broadcasters. Translation of the presentation material had to be arranged and its length estimated so that in each country (and making allowances for the likelihood that, for example, the text in German would last longer than its Italian counterpart), the presentation would take just about as long as that of the originating broadcaster. Thanks to the extraordinary improvisatory skills of the multilingual presenters, things seldom went badly wrong. And it was ironic that, on the only occasion when they did, there was no language problem for the BBC. The broadcast came from Chicago, when, on 2 October 1980, Georg Solti conducted a fine and very high-powered performance of Mahler's Eighth Symphony, 'Symphony of a Thousand'. I had sent ahead my gifted colleague Leo Black to help and advise the American broadcasting staff. But to no avail: somewhere down the line an anonymous technician, perhaps presuming that no symphony could possibly last for more than an hour, had thrown a vital switch and Valerie Solti, listening at home in Primrose Hill, suddenly heard two separate commercials emanating from her stereo speakers. In the concert audience myself I was unaware of what had happened until, in the control cubicle afterwards, I found Leo professionally distraught. But such accidents were extremely rare and another American origination when, in 1982, Giulini broadcast a programme of Webern, Berg (the Violin Concerto with Perlman) and Bruckner from Los Angeles, was trouble-free and memorable.

My dealings with the EBU, in which I had the superb support of Tony Dean, the senior member of EBU staff dedicated to international musical matters, were the icing on the cake of domestic affairs which – to pursue a culinary metaphor and a famous *Punch* joke – had been "excellent in parts". The best parts, obviously, were the Proms, orchestral matters and day-to-day dealings not only with civilised and congenial musician colleagues, but also with young aspiring musicians who sought my advice and, no doubt, support. Two such were George Benjamin, who came to see me in August 1978, and Evelyn Glennie who, in February 1985, astonished me by causing me within a few minutes to forget that she was profoundly deaf. George and I established a nice, sometimes silly relationship based upon the Benjamin-Ponsonby Rules, of which there is really only one: neither is obliged to respond to any communication from the other.

And of course I met many eminent, older musicians.

In May 1973 I had been able to send my brother, Nigel Jaques, a postcard from Italy –

> In five days I have spent 24 hours with the Waltons on Ischia, an afternoon with Henze, a few minutes with Berio, a twinkling with Dallapiccola – and I am, after all, travelling with Boulez! Tour going well.

The tour proceeded from Rome, via Florence and Venice, to Vienna, where I was lucky to find time to see Weill's *Mahagonny*, *Rosenkavalier* with Lisa Della Casa, and Berg's *Lulu* with Anja Silja – all at the Staatsoper.

Some cherries on the icing on the cake.

# 15

## Canterbury

"I'm sorry to say that Canterbury is not only a very small place, but also a very parochial one."

The speaker was Robert Runcie, Archbishop of Canterbury. I had found myself next to him in the queue for hats and coats after a formal dinner at the Royal Festival Hall. I was planning my second Canterbury Festival (1988) and was having fundraising problems of which, introducing myself, I told him. He was courteous and sympathetic.

I had welcomed my appointment as Artistic Director of the Festival. In its latest format it was just three years old and in 1987 I inherited a 'British' theme. This I thought too broad, so I narrowed it to 'English', with special emphasis upon the English language. Relevant talks were given by Alan Bennett who, in the three decades or so since *Beyond the Fringe*, had become a famous writer; by Robert Burchfield, author of a guide to spoken English; by the playwright Christopher Fry; and by Cormac Rigby, my erstwhile colleague at the BBC who, as Radio 3's Presentation Editor, and himself a familiar voice, had established good practice for presenters, but whose post was later done away with – the consequences now all too embarrassingly obvious. As well as talks there were of course plays: *Twelfth Night* and *She Stoops to Conquer* came from a company whose casts included John Curry, better known as a champion skater, and Ian Lavender, immortalised as Pike (Captain Mainwaring's "stupid boy") in *Dad's Army*. Particularly welcome was Timothy West, who had prepared for the Festival a programme derived from Bernard Shaw's trenchant music criticism (he wrote as 'Corno di Bassetto'). Another actor was Alec McCowen who at the Opening Service read Hamlet's advice to the players, Archbishop Thomas's speech at the end of the first part of *Murder in the Cathedral*, poems by George Herbert and Milton and, finally, John Betjeman's *Diary of a Church Mouse*. The anthem, *May Sion receive me*, was by Judith Weir, a 'featured' composer whose opera *A Night at the Chinese Opera* – original, witty and funny – was, in Kent Opera's brilliant production, a highlight of the Festival.

Another was the Opening Concert, at which BBC forces under Richard Armstrong gave a programme of which I was proud:

Tallis: Spem in alium (the BBC Singers)
Vaughan Williams: Fantasia on a Theme of Thomas Tallis
Tippett: The Vision of St Augustine [the first Archbishop of Canterbury]

Michael was present and wrote to me afterwards, "What a marvellous concert! The great Tallis had me soon in tears of joy [...] Thanks and love, Michael"

An unscheduled highlight of a different kind assailed the Festival on the evening of Thursday 15 October. Theatregoers to the Marlowe Theatre (Kent Opera's *The Magic Flute*) and the Gulbenkian Theatre (Medieval Players' *Sturdy Beggars*) emerged into a strong and hostile wind – the beginning of the "hurricane" which Michael Fish had endearingly failed to forecast. The wind blew all night, not gusting, but with fierce unvarying violence. Dawn brought a remission and the discovery of much serious damage to roofs and trees. I like to think it was true that the only building to escape was the Cathedral.

Miraculously, the telephone system was working. But it brought me only bad news. Imogen Cooper, due to give a recital that evening and staying in the country nearby, was cut off by fallen trees; the Steinway she was to play was immobilised on the motorway; its tuner was stuck in Brighton. And there was no light or heating. It didn't seem likely that the recital would take place or that, if it did, anybody much would come. However, after nail-biting hours, power was restored, piano and tuner found their separate ways, as did Imogen and a modest but attentive audience which she congratulated on their loyal hardihood. Then she played Bach, Schubert (the D major Sonata D.850) and Schumann (*Davidsbündlertänze*). I had never before – and have never since – heard her play Bach, but the French Suite in G, BWV 816, was very lucid and its dances danced elegantly. Earlier she had played Mozart's E flat Concerto, K.271, with Jane Glover and the London Mozart Players – a robust performance, by no means ladylike. Between concerto and recital she took authoritative, and humorous, masterclasses in the Gulbenkian Theatre, as did dear, inarticulate John Ogdon, whose towering performance of the Liszt Sonata in his own recital was unforgettable, and all the more so since it followed the Brahms Paganini Variations, technically a major Himalayan peak.

The range of music heard at the 1987 Festival covered six centuries – from Henry VIII, the composer, to George Benjamin, the composer/conductor, not yet 30, whose massive *Jubilation*, for schools orchestras and choirs was given in the Cathedral. (The welcoming squeals of the choirs, when George took his place, can be heard on the Radio 3 recording.) Quite different, but just as enjoyable, was the concert by Django Bates's very young and very Big Band, Loose Tubes, a concert noticeably well patronised by King's School students. Yes, it was a good Festival.

121

Planning the next one along the same lines, I invited Nicholas Maw to be our 'resident' composer and Nicholas Cleobury, with Eileen Hulse and Aquarius, gave a fine performance of his beautiful *La Vita Nuova*. I also featured Messiaen, whose tremendous *Et exspecto resurrectionem mortuorum*, with the BBC Symphony Orchestra under Oliver Knussen, rattled the Cathedral's rood screen, while at the other end of the Messiaenic scale Peter Donohoe, with three gifted colleagues, gave us the touching *Quatuor pour la Fin du Temps*. Messiaen the organist was featured by Thomas Trotter with *Messe de la Pentecôte* in his recital and Nicholas Maw's *Essay* preceded Liszt's *Fantasia and Fugue on the name BACH* in Allan Wicks's. Peter Hurford's magisterial Bach programme demonstrated a combination – trumpet and reed – of very striking character which Peter told me was "one of my specialities". Of Sena Jurinac's superb masterclasses I have written elsewhere.

After the English Language in 1987 I had settled for Stories and Story-telling as a very loosely binding theme. Among those who gave germane talks were Richard Hoggart ('Stories in my Life') and Jonathan Miller ('Stories in the Theatre') who delivered, I rather think, a largely improvised narrative – the gift of the gab? – which was nevertheless rich in intelligent insight. I very much liked "When you go to the doctor, you are auditioning to be a patient", which wittily connected his two professional lives.

So I was pleased – by and large – with the music and talks programmes. But the theatre programme was a pig's ear, for reasons beyond my control. My chairman, Peter Williams, without telling (let alone consulting) me, had handed to the Marlowe Theatre management responsibility for what was seen there during the Festival. Moreover, I was obliged – for local/political reasons – to accommodate, for example, an amateur company which presented, in Whitstable's Playhouse,

122

*The Importance of Being Earnest*, a masterpiece way beyond any but accomplished professionals. Williams was also unwilling to tell me whether he was simply chairman, or executive chairman; and there is a world of difference. So, perhaps inevitably, we had a blistering row (which really is not my scene) and it became crystal clear to me that the mismatch of personality and, more importantly, of policy was intolerable. When, at a Festival committee meeting, I heard a representative of the University say, "Car boot sales are very big. We should have car boot sales in the Festival", I knew that I was at the end of this particular road... and that Archbishop Runcie had been right.

Afterthought: to let off steam, I wrote a rather jejune burlesque which is printed below. I hasten to say that, though Max Wall could not match Ken Dodd's astounding range and stamina, he was very good at what he did – which did not, though, belong in my Festival programme.

All things bright and beautiful
All features great and small
All things warm and wonderful
– the Chairman wants Max Wall.

Each little show that opens
Each little choir that sings
He modifies their programmes
And takes away their stings.
All things...

The rich man at Leeds Castle
The poor man on Burgate
He woos them all and orders
Their demographic state.

123

All things…

The Cs and Ds he favours
The lowly and the poor
He combs the slums and byways
For more and more and more.
All things…

Alf Garnett as the Miser
Can never be surpassed
At Twelfth Night with Vanessa
He clearly is aghast
All things…

The lofty-browed Director
Has tastes for As and Bs
The Chairman will not have it
"Down market!" he decrees.
All things…

He dotes upon processions
On fireworks and on fun
He's going into training
For Sunday morning's Run.

All things paradoxical
At this Arts Festival
Ponsonby wants Messiaen*
THE CHAIRMAN WANTS MAX WALL!

---

* or Mahler or Mozart

# 16

## At the "Musben"

In the January 1997 issue of *Scherzo*, the newsletter of the Musicians Benevolent Fund (now Help Musicians UK), I wrote a valedictory piece after ten years of part-time work. It is self-explanatory:

All good things come to an end.

On 30 June I said a sad farewell to the MBF – the "Musben" in Ursula Vaughan Williams's nice elision. My association went back to 1972 when my job at the BBC carried with it ex-officio membership of the Executive Committee. Its chairman then was that great and good (also courteously formidable) man, Thomas Armstrong, who had once accompanied me in an Oxford recital in the late '40s. A later chairman was Ian Hunter, with whom I had worked at the Edinburgh Festival in the '50s. When I left the BBC, in 1985, Ian asked me to write a report on the feasibility of establishing Friends of the MBF. I concluded that Friends were viable – but I did not anticipate my own involvement. So it was a happy surprise when Martin Williams asked me to become the Friends' first administrator.

With Alison Evans I set to. We assembled 26 mailing-lists and sent off thousands of leaflets featuring Dame Janet Baker, Evelyn Glennie, Dame Vera Lynn, Sir Geraint Evans, Bob Geldof, Sir Alexander Gibson, Nigel Kennedy, John Ogdon, Courtney Pine and Simon Rattle. The response was pathetic: in that first year, 1987, we mustered about 350 members. But we persisted. Our first newsletter – a crude affair – appeared in July and in November we organised our first auction. Thanks to the generosity of donors, we made £23,000. The most valuable lots came from Harrison Birtwistle, Otto Klemperer's daughter Lotte, and Evelyn Barbirolli, who gave us Kathleen Ferrier's own copy of Gluck's *Orfeo*, the last work she sang before her final illness. Other gifts included a signed photograph of Brahms, an oil painting by Sir Henry Wood and a ticket for one of Haydn's Salomon concerts which I had picked up in a junk shop and which fetched £350. In May 1988 we held our first Friends Annual Gathering at Lambeth. In June the Northern Sinfonia gave a concert for us in Newcastle – the first of a number given outside London by sympathetic managements. That autumn we sold our first Christmas card. All this activity – and a great deal of hard work – contributed to a steady increase in membership and an improvement in the newsletter, which we re-christened *Scherzo* in 1992.

By this time – and thanks to the industry of Hilary Pentycross, who had succeeded Alison Evans in March 1989 – Christmas card sales (including that small masterpiece, Quentin Blake's 'Love Duet') had multiplied many times. In 1995 sales had risen to 111,000 and membership had peaked at 1,745. In other words the Friends were doing what they had been established to do: to propagate knowledge of the Fund, raise its profile (particularly outside London and the South-East) and inspire support for its work. Hilary took over the Friends in January 1994, while I remained editor of *Scherzo*. Grand plans were in the offing: a second auction (which raised £21,000) and Simon Caradoc Evans's amazing brain-child, the Mega Concert. In my own mind there was another project – the one which at first we called the "multi-music concert", but which turned out to be the MBF's 75th Birthday Concert.

In my report about the feasibility of a Friends organisation I had written, "The Fund should surely consider an occasional event including a number of groups – symphonic, 'light', jazz, pop, country and so on." Though myself a passionate lover of 'classical' music, I was convinced that the MBF should manifest its interest in all kinds of musicians – specially young ones – not only those epitomised by the Royal Concert and the symphony concerts and the many organ recitals which the Friends were arranging. Slowly the idea began to take root and after much understandable hesitation the Executive Committee gave me a somewhat guarded go-ahead.

We encountered some enormous difficulties. Hard to come by were sponsorship and celebrated soloists for Malcolm Arnold's *Toy Symphony*. (Among those who were unavailable were Sting, Shirley Bassey, Tommy Steele, Humphrey Lyttelton and Elvis Costello!) Impossible to come by was a broadcast. But, thanks to the wonderfully generous musicians and to behind-the-scene helpers like Lady Solti and Lois Sieff, the concert memorably succeeded. Not all of our regular supporters cared for Django Bates's contribution, but it was exciting to hear the shouts of approval from a new audience – young people mostly, who were probably encountering the MBF for the first time in their lives. Having pioneered the concert, I heaved a huge sigh of relief when it was over and a profit of £11,000 declared.

Looking back on nearly 25 years of association and nearly 10 years of formal involvement with the MBF I recall with special admiration Pat Sharland's warmth and her passionate concern for the beneficiaries, Jan Lowy's courteous mastery of the Fund's publicity and of the Royal Concert, and Martin Williams's fastidious integrity. They set golden examples – which is not to denigrate their successors. Times change, as do methods and style. The old Friends Advisory Committee, which spoke the language of the music profession (I refuse to call it the music industry, as is fashionable), is now replaced by the Friends and Events Committee, whose members are mostly

127

impressive and influential media-people. They will no doubt see to it that the Friends flourish again – for, sadly. membership has recently declined. In the summer of 1992 Hilary circulated a professionally prepared questionnaire to the Friends. The response was substantial and it told us pretty clearly what they expected from the administration. I urge those concerned to re-read it and I dare to offer them some well-meant advice. Recruitment and retention of Friends must be managed in as humanly personal a way as possible. (I remember topping, tailing and, where appropriate, PS-ing thousands of letters to potential members.) Friends must be cherished, listened to and, when feasible, their suggestions adopted. And they must be thanked. If they cannot have their own newsletter, then the Fund's newsletter should surely carry a section devoted to their affairs. For they are friends in every sense – musicians and music-lovers who have made a public commitment to the work of the "Musben". They are a constituency of great value and potential influence. And, as Dr Johnson said, their friendship must be kept "in constant repair".

# 17

## Teaching and Talking

I am not a born teacher, but some very spasmodic teaching has come my way. I fear that none of my pupils gained much from my schooling.

The first were some Scots Guardsmen – my own platoon. An 'education' period was ordered and I decided to read to my lot. I had recently finished Evelyn Waugh's *Brideshead Revisited*, which had been published in 1945. I was still under its spell and I thought I would try it out on my soldiers. But, though it dealt with soldiery, it was by any standards very sophisticated and I decided that I would pair it with something very simple – and I wish I could remember whether it was *The Wind in the Willows* or *Winnie the Pooh* that I chose. Having read, I invited comments. But not many came back. My soldiers, after all, were enjoying a restful period. They were not on guard duty. They were not square-bashing. So they were not sharply attentive; indeed they tended, quite politely, to snooze. Who shall blame them?

In 1950 the Oxford University Opera Club put on Berlioz's *The Trojans* and my friend Royd Barker was chorus-master for the production. He was then in charge of music at Abingdon Grammar School and because the dual commitments were unduly heavy he got permission to bring in some extra teaching help. Though wholly unqualified, I joined him. But very soon I too got involved in *The Trojans*. However, between us, Royd and I provided the boys with enough time if – in my case – not much talent.

Things did not go well for me. There is nothing more trying than attempting to teach an unwilling class of boys how to enjoy class-singing *from behind an upright piano*: you can't see them. And what I was hearing was hardly harmonious. But it was obvious that there was one particularly truculent boy who was infecting the rest. So I told him to deliver 100 (maybe 200) lines by Monday. He failed to do so. I gave him an extension till Wednesday. He failed again. At my wits' end, I asked the Headmaster, James Cobban, for his advice. It was instant and uncompromising: "Flog him." Now I had been flogged – let's say 'beaten' – at Eton by my head of house, but I had never beaten anybody. I didn't know how hard to hit. But the deed had to be done and I fetched a cane from the Senior Common Room, whose occupants learned of my errand with relish. Then I sought out the boy – let's call him Connolly (Evelyn Waugh's choice for a troublesome family and apparently a dig at the literary critic Cyril Connolly). But we traipsed in vain round the school searching for an unoccupied room. There was none. Then I had an irreligious brainwave – the capacious organ loft in the school chapel. And there I delivered six of the best, whether too hard or too soft I had no idea. In any case Connolly did not cry out or complain. But if his behaviour improved, I am doubtful. Today, of course, his parents would have sued the school and I should have been sacked, possibly imprisoned.

Indeed when, more than thirty years later, I described this incident to the head teacher of a primary school where I had offered some part-time help with reading she was very shocked – but I took some classes nevertheless. The children (some of the girls hardly children any more) were fascinated by their new teacher. I talked posh and was immensely tall. They needed to know my height and my size of shoe. But we got on pretty well considering the social and educational chasm which existed between me and the white, Asian and black children I was in charge of. Indeed I'm fairly sure that one or two of the (pubescent) black girls gave me the glad eye. But the discovery that not one of them had been read to by a mum, or dad, or gran, dismayed me. Be that as it may, I have happy recollections of a Church of England school, whose head teacher was a Roman Catholic and many of whose pupils were not Christian. Wholly admirable was the practice whereby the school regularly visited the nearby C of E church, the non-Christian children handing out prayer-books and hymn-books at the back. Would that adult international bodies would adopt the same tolerant enlightenment as that exhibited by Emmanuel Primary School in Mill Lane, West Hampstead.

More important than my primitive teaching was my time as a NADFAS (National Association of Decorative & Fine Arts Societies) lecturer. This body is quietly successful and represents a very large constituency of retired persons, most of them female. There are societies all over Britain (I lectured in Lockerbie, before the ghastly jumbo disaster, and in Devon) and the organisation is run by tyrannical ladies from a London office. These ladies insist upon an audition and, though not a 'fine arts' man, I passed mine, giving them a five-minute snatch from a talk – not yet written – about the Proms. This talk proved popular with the societies and it soon took on a fixed format: I began with the occasion when, on 7 August 1974, Thomas Allen, the baritone in Carl Orff's *Carmina Burana*, fainted.

It was a hot night, made hotter by the presence of TV cameras, and it gradually became clear that Allen was not well: he was swaying around and, before long, sat down and slumped back in his chair. Miraculously, André Previn kept the music going while Allen's (possibly lifeless) body was removed. A whispered conversation between Previn and Gerald English, the tenor soloist, rightly suggested that he would try to take over the baritone's solos. Meanwhile, in the

131

Arena, a student singer, who was studying Allen's role and had the music with him, saw his chance. Nobody has ever run faster than he to the backstage area where he told a BBC colleague, "I know the baritone part. I have the music. You have to let me go on. You have no alternative." So on he went, in a purple roll-top sweater and jeans. Imagine Previn's feelings. Who was this young man? An anarchist? A baritone-poisoner? But he had the music – so perhaps could sing the role. He could. And he did. His name was Patrick McCarthy and, though he had a decent career, he was never so famous again.

Next night, the Promenaders delivered one of their very wittiest 'shouts' – "A Promenader has fainted. Would one of the soloists please take his place!"

The other book-end of my Proms talk was an anecdote about the Clarinet Concerto by that admirable Scottish composer (who has, like Peter Racine Fricker, chosen to live in the USA), Thea Musgrave. The work is interesting and unusual in that the soloist moves from time to time to another designated part of the orchestra, where he – in this case Gervase de Peyer – finds a music stand with the appropriate music. But once (at rehearsal I have to suppose) Gervase made the appropriate move – to the brass section. The music stand was there all right, but no music – just a message which read "Bugger off!"

I thought it best not to deliver this punchline at the end of a talk I gave in Alnwick in January 1999. A friend and contemporary, Bill Hugonin, who had been agent to the Duke of Northumberland, told me that Alnwick Music Society would welcome a talk based upon the programmes *The Mysterious Art of the Conductor* I had made for the BBC's World Service in 1986. The Playhouse, an erstwhile cinema cleverly converted for concerts, modest dramatics and talks, proved an ideal auditorium. I played music examples on tape and I had a lovely audience, interested and responsive. Afterwards, there were drinks in a very friendly gathering of all and sundry: I liked very much the Dowager Duchess and the local organist, to whom I gave the stick (baton) with which I had, presumptuously, illustrated some of the notorious traps (the Scherzo of Dvořák 7, the start of Strauss's *Don Juan*) a conductor encounters.

Less successful was a talk which, in the event, I did *not* give in Lincoln on 12 December 1986. I was part of a hotel 'package'. So I was, in theory, guaranteed an audience. No such luck. Just before I was due 'on' I went to the hotel loo (as one does) and there encountered a pleasant man who asked if I was the lecturer. Learning that I was, he told me he was the local music critic and was much looking forward to hearing me. But he turned out to be my only listener, so we spent the evening drinking whisky together. He was a nice man.

The occasional fiasco apart, I have enjoyed holding forth. I guess I am fond of the sound of my own voice.

# 18

## Competitions and Scholarships

I have never done jury service in a court of law but less fortunate friends have generally told me they endured much boredom and some disgust. Above all, they said, the sheer unintelligent mediocrity of the accused persons was deeply dispiriting. Happily, the young musicians I have listened to, as a juror, were almost never unintelligent or uninteresting.

My first experience in this field came in 1974, when Ernest Warburton – then the BBC's Head of Music in Manchester – invited me to chair a national piano competition at Lancaster University. I gladly agreed, my fellow-jurors including Ernest himself, Vlado Perlemuter, the renowned Chopinist who had played to Ravel every note he had written for piano, and the redoubtable Fanny Waterman – not yet a Dame but already displaying damely characteristics: she took me aside and explained how she expected me to conduct our deliberations. I held my peace. But – for whatever reason – we eventually made a mistake. The two best competitors were Yitkin Seow, a Singaporean not yet 20, and Philip Fowke, then 24. Both were clearly very gifted, but I (and other jurors) found Fowke's Schumann too mannered, so we gave the prize to Seow and – as is so often the case – it was not he, but Fowke, who made the bigger career (and became, long afterwards, a dear friend).

Three years later – and no doubt 'ex officio' – I was invited to join the jury of the Arthur Rubinstein International Piano Master Competition, held in Tel Aviv and Jerusalem. I found myself in very grand company: the pianists on the jury included Jacques Février, Rudolf Firkušný and Nikita Magaloff. Though listed, Michelangeli did not turn up, perhaps predictably. But the event was rich in incident – and an accident or two. One tiny incident tickled me. Before a big formal dinner, the guests (at various tables) were awaiting Rubinstein himself and Daniel Barenboim's father, Enrique, spotted me at a nearby table. He came across and we chatted about pianistic matters. But at one point, while still speaking, he reached up (like his eminent son, he was a small man) and straightened my tie. Silly and trivial, I know, but unforgettable.

Less trivial were two incidents involving Golda Meir, who had been Israel's prime minister. At the end of the competition the organisers remembered – rather too late in the day – that the twelve judges had to sign the certificates of the twelve finalists, a total of 144 signatures. We were hustled into a smallish room with rather too few smallish tables. The certificates were scrolls, rolled up, and the only way to sign such a document is to unroll it with the elbows and to sign it, writing more or less upside-down. This was going on, amid some giggling, when Mrs Meir walked in. We all stood up deferentially – and the scrolls rolled themselves up with soft 'phuts'. Not all got signed. Later that day, at the final concert with the Israel Philharmonic, the judges were lined up on one side of the conductor, Eliahu Inbal, the finalists on the other. The proceedings were introduced by Mrs Meir who, in a speech rather lacking in musical insight, found it necessary to refer to the Holocaust, a reference made the more insensitive by the fact that the competition winner was the 24-year-old German musician Gerhard Oppitz, who had to cope, a few minutes later, with the towering problems of the Brahms B flat Concerto. Cope he did, with great technical assurance, and I thought him a worthy winner, his fellow-competitors including Pierre-Laurent Aimard and Yitkin Seow, whose very natural

135

musicianship had impressed me at Lancaster, as it now had Rubinstein, who made him a personal award.

Returning to London I found a proposal from the Rupert Foundation (whose background resources came from tobacco) that the BBC collaborate in the organisation of a competitive event for young conductors. I agreed to provide the services of the BBC Symphony Orchestra and assembled an impressive group of adjudicators – Gennadi Rozhdestvensky, David Atherton, Manoug Parikian, Antony Hopkins and Malcolm Williamson, already Master of the Queen's Music. In April 1978 we spent three days listening to a number of not especially interesting young conductors. But Andrew Litton impressed us: he avoided the usual traps – in dealing with transposing instruments particularly – and addressed the Orchestra with sensible modesty. At one point he encountered the Orchestra's principal horn, whose natural conversational style and whose contempt for the whole breed of conductors verged on the savage. But Alan Civil could – and did – play like an angel. Nevertheless, the following exchange took place between the two: "Principal Horn, at letter D, could you please play a fraction earlier?" "Could you conduct a fraction earlier?" Not an angelic response.

Not long after leaving the BBC at the end of 1985, I was approached by Tony Wingate of the Harold Hyam Wingate Foundation which, he told me, was planning to establish scholarships in various fields including, rather particularly, music. Would I involve myself? Without then knowing much about Tony or his organisation, I jumped at the suggestion, having come to believe that, though prizes can be useful, there are serious risks attached (notably over-exposure), whereas scholarships, by their nature, are likely to be low-key and slow-burn. I soon found the Wingate Scholarships were themselves low-key: they gave away very substantial sums of money but did not look for publicity – though it was no doubt welcome when it came their way.

The scheme got going in 1988 and was to last for twenty-three years, though my own participation ended in 2008. The work involved listening to a considerable number of tapes, weeding them down to a dozen or so, auditioning (or sometimes – when the applicant was, for example, writing a book about Janáček – just interviewing), then, in privacy, adjudicating. In this I had the help at various times of, among others, Tom Hemsley, Jill Gomez, Catherine Wilson, Thea King and – in his own personal and peculiar way – my erstwhile BBC colleague Robert Layton. Voluminously knowledgeable about Scandinavian music, Bob was also a master-spoofer, his *chef d'oeuvre* an entry in Grove's august Dictionary of Music and Musicians recording the life and works of the Danish flautist, conductor and composer Dag Esrum-Hellerup (1803–1891), every word pure fiction. It is said – and one can believe it – that Stanley Sadie, overall editor of Grove, was volcanically angry when he discovered the fabrication.

Wingate Scholarship auditions were a pleasure for reasons other than musical: they were generally held in the Craxton Studios, a big Hampstead house with a high, spacious music room looking out onto lilacs and rhododendrons. The room naturally contained a concert grand. A lovely bonus was a number of the paintings by John Craxton – soft-coloured, linearly outlined, often self-evidently Greek in setting; sometimes, if the music-making was dull, my eye drifted gratefully towards them. (I hope it is true, incidentally, that John's sister Janet, a fine oboist, joined the Royal Opera House Orchestra in order to play *Figaro*.)

Our audition procedure was to ask the young musician to introduce him- or herself and the accompanist. We would then introduce ourselves and I would invite any pianist to try the piano, whose action was on the heavy side. After twenty minutes of music the musician would join us for an informal interview. This was often revealing. Some of the applicants appeared to have no money at all and these were often the most warm-hearted and humorous. Once, a young tenor startled and enchanted us with the statement that, "I am almost certainly the grandson of Heddle Nash." (It emerged that his grandmother had been generous with her favours, the eminent Heddle Nash among her lovers.)

Wingate Scholarships celebrated their twentieth birthday in 2008 with a concert at the Wigmore Hall, the artists – all past Scholars – Elizabeth Watts, Kishani Jayasinghe, Ronan Collett and Simon Lepper. The scheme was discontinued three years later after awarding 174 music scholarships out of a total of over 1000 in subjects as diverse as Medical Research and Education. At risk of invidiousness I name Andrew Kennedy, Jacques Imbrailo, Amy Dickson, Catrin Wyn-Davies, Julian Perkins and Chi-Yu Mo, who joined the clarinet section of the LSO soon after completing his Scholarship, as successful past Scholars.

My involvement as the Scholarships' Music Adviser was very rewarding – and it gave me the greatest pleasure over the best part of twenty years: Tony Wingate was admirably 'hands-on' and the award of the Scholarships was arranged in a manner both wholly professional and also agreeably informal.

# 19

## An Abortive Campaign

Just as I have always been fussy about the mounting and framing of pictures, I have cared even more intensely about the broadcast presentation of music – the framing of it.

In September 1975 there was a meeting of the International Music Council, hosted by the Canadian Music Council in Toronto, and I gave a talk on 'The Presentation of Music on Radio'. A long talk printed in the Canada Music Book, 1976, I give here only a tiny part of my final paragraph – "presentation, a broadcasting art in itself and one to which it would be impossible to devote too much meticulous and committed concern".

On and off, I have been banging on about this issue for more than a quarter of a century. In December 2007 *Classical Music* magazine published an open letter to Roger Wright, then the fairly new Controller, Radio 3:

Dear Roger

The other day I ventured, in a live Radio 3 programme about a superb concert by the BBC Symphony Orchestra and Pierre Boulez, to voice some criticism of R3's current presentation style. (Should I return my fee? It was very modest.)

But what I said brought me some letters strongly endorsing my views, so I am emboldened to write this 'open' letter to you. I dare say it won't come as a surprise, since I have written to you and to one or two of your colleagues before now.

I guess that your presenters are encouraged to be informal, chatty, even matey, so that the accidental listener to R3 is not put off by 'posh' accents, 'highbrow' statements, a lofty manner. As a result, I fear that listeners of ordinary intelligence are talked down to. For example, a (female) presenter told us recently, 'it was the slow movement that stole my heart away': a sick-bag, please.

There is, of course, no 'typical' listener. Better, though, to talk up to him (or, *passim*, her); to give him the information he needs both before and after the relay. And what he needs is the title of the work, the name of its composer, the identity of the artist or artists concerned. (If there is time, more information, particularly dates.) These days listening to R3 resembles a guessing game. Sometimes none of this information is given in advance (the 'innocent ear' approach); sometimes the composer but not the work (or vice versa) is named; sometimes the performers are identified only in a back announcement. Disgracefully, the other day, the singer of a Wolf group was named before the relay, the accompanist not till after it. That was ill-mannered and unprofessional.

It should go without saying that pronunciation (even of Baltic and Balkan names, of which, nowadays, we hear an awful lot) should be correct.

At least as important, though, is the question of value judgments, the personal opinions of presenters about particular works or performances. One of my correspondents recalled that when the inimitable Tom Crowe, in a back announcement, said, 'I thought that was a wonderful performance', irate Third Programme listeners rang in to demand he be put in his place.

Of course, times have changed – and R3 is, alas, by no means the Third Programme – but it really is not the job of the presenter to evaluate the work or the performance. That is presumptuous and very irritating: listeners prefer, and should be entitled, to make up their own minds. (And, of course, performances are always 'fantastic', 'glorious', 'mind-blowing' – never plodding or badly balanced.)

The oral style of some (male) presenters seems self-consciously characterful. (My correspondent described them as 'ego-trippers'.) But there is also a practical problem here: if the voice soars and swoops, at the lowest level it may be inaudible to the listener whose circumstances are not ideal – e.g. if he is driving. Simple, measured comprehensibility, avoiding extremes of level, is what is needed.

140

And what you need is a music presentation editor, somebody who would emulate the late, great Cormac Rigby (in whose time, incidentally – because the ear needs a moment to switch from music to speech – it was axiomatic that back announcements never began with a name) supervising presentation according to agreed, rigorous guidelines. This would not preclude friendliness, as anyone who remembers Tom Crowe, Patricia Hughes, Tony Scotland or Cormac himself will confirm. [...]

Meanwhile, cherish Radio 3 – it *is* the jewel in the BBC's somewhat tarnished crown – and enjoy running the Proms. There is no better job in music.

All very good wishes
Robert

Six years later, I wrote to Roger again:

Dear Roger,

You will be surprised, perhaps pleased (perhaps quite indifferent) to have this letter – because it is to tell you that I have resolved never again to write to you in censorious terms.

Why? Well, my previous letters haven't had the smallest influence. And I don't want to become even more of a boring back number. But *particularly* because you have a lot of much more important stuff on your plate.

Specifically: you aren't going to appoint a Music Presentation Editor while making colleagues redundant.

But before signing off, I want to make some points which are surely important.

First, your listeners are at home, or in a car, where there are many distractions – so clarity and repetition (i.e. before *and* after a work/programme) are essential. So is diction. [...]

Second, listeners always need to know what they are going to hear – and who the artists are. It is deplorable that the accompanist of a Lieder recital (or just one song) is sometimes not named. And that a concerto soloist *is* named, but not, sometimes, the conductor and/or orchestra. That is an insult to those musicians.

Third, relevant information. For example, the listener should *surely* be told that in Bach's Second Orchestral Suite there is a solo flute. And that the Overture to Mozart's *Don Giovanni* goes straight into Leporello's aria; whereas the concert ending (I don't know whose) is a contrivance. *Both*, recent omissions.

Fourth, gushing amateurishness. I don't need, or want, to be told that Sibelius 5 is "exquisitely beautiful". (Indeed, *is* it?) Nor that I would shortly hear Chopin's Nocturne No. 3 – no opus, no key – so which was it going to be?

Fifth, pronunciation. Little things – like "Hoogo", *not* "Hewgo" Wolf. And very big, awful things like "Sawltsberg". (Sack that presenter, *please*.)

Sixth, please settle for short-o opus: we don't go to the ōpera, do we?

Seventh, a small piece of Good Practice. More than 25 years ago, when Cormac Rigby was the admirable Mus. Pres. Ed., it was agreed – *and* observed – that back announcements would *never* begin with a name: the ear needs a moment to adjust from music to speech (even more so when the name is Baltic and strange).

Finally, what I suppose is a lost cause – the *invariable* broadcast of complete works. Presenters now often tell me that we will shortly hear, say, the 'New World' Symphony – but we *actually* hear only one movement. This is misleading, not to say dishonest: certainly deplorable. [...]

If you are still with me, Roger, I am grateful. You will fairly observe that my listening hours are limited. So what? Am I an inferior listener? (In a way I am: you offload most of your Baltic and Balkan EBU recordings during my listening hours!)

Some of the above can be found on p. 175 of my book, *Musical Heroes*, of which, my spy tells me, you have a copy. But, if he is wrong, I will very gladly present you with one over another lunch at the RIBA. You deserve lunch anyway – and it would be a pleasure. [...]

All very best wishes with your current struggles
Robert

P.S. I enclose, against the advice of Helen Wallace, who said it tasted like sour grapes, a spoof which, if you take it amiss, will no doubt rule out *any* lunch, *ever*.

The spoof referred to I sent to a few friends, colleagues and one or two journalists. Among them was Charles Moore who, in *The Spectator*, had voiced some sympathetic views about presentation on Radio 3. His acknowledgement delighted me: 'I found [the spoof] very unconvincing because the English in which it is written is far too good." Here is the spoof:

From:       Condoner, Radio 3
To:         Radio 3 Presenters
Subject:    The human voice of Radio 3
cc.         Chief Assistant, Extravagant Epithets
            Chief Assistant, Baltic and Balkan
            Special Editor, Very Obscure Composers
            Special Advisor, Ocarinas, Jews' Harps, Swanee Whistles
            Very Special Advisor, Comedy Guests and Stand-Ups

You will perhaps be aware of some recent public criticism of our Channel's oral style and I want to assure you that you have my support in what you are doing – and saying. Indeed I commend the cosy mateyness which many of you so effortlessly achieve.

By and large the criticism, mostly about morning programmes, is pedantic, our critics elderly sticklers stuck in a Reithian time-warp. They maintain that listeners need detailed identification of a work and its performers before and after any relay. But if we were to do this our airtime would be cluttered with names, numbers, keys and instrumental (or vocal) minutiae, our commentaries dry-as-dust.

There is also some criticism of our pronunciation. As if it mattered! For example, the distinction between (Salz)burg and (Alban) Berg is a nicety important only to academics. Radio 3 is not a university. It is perhaps a bazaar (OD definition: 'a large shop selling fancy goods').

Some critics object to the personalization of our presentation and to self-reference by presenters. But this humanizes what we do! To know that a presenter had "goosebumps" when listening to a specially thrilling performance paints for the listener a picture of a touchingly vibrant personality – a welcome contrast to the cool detachment of an earlier generation of presenters. Nor should personal reaction be curbed: "Wow!" is a concise and expressive response.

Presenters will not go far wrong if they emulate Classic FM. To believe that 'great' works are so fragile that they will not survive being broken up is to be ridiculously purist. In any case our live broadcasts surely cater for the minority who protest that they need to hear the whole work in one unbroken (and surely often indigestible) sequence.

The New Generation listener (to whom we must constantly reach out) wants only the general picture: he/she is likely to be busy, focused on an iPad, Googling and Tweeting. The late Hans Keller attached importance to "the quality of the listening" – a concept now patently absurd. (The bonnet of the not yet late Robert Ponsonby accommodates a monstrous swarm of similar bees.) So: never mind about keys or Köchels – "And now a morsel of Mozart" is a charming presentational gambit. Today's Radio 3 presenters should be chatty, chummy, random: no drab consistency, please. Stimulate your listeners, surprise, even bewilder them. Our motto should be 'Keep Listeners On Their Toes' (KLOTT).

We should be at least as well known for the wonderfully human accessibility of our presenters as for the quality of the music presented.

ROGER WRONG
Condoner, Radio 3

In the summer of 2014 *The Oldie* – perhaps an apt forum – published a RANT along the same lines.

But, after nearly forty years, I am conscious that I have not had the smallest influence upon presentation style and methods on Radio 3. It is still often unhelpful and uninformative – indeed amateurish.

144

# 20

## Handel

My first serious encounter with Handel came in 1954 when Jack Phipps, who was later to make a fine career as an administrator, suggested that we should put on a production of *Semele*, which is surely unique in Handel's output as combining comedy – indeed, quite sexy comedy – with the choral aspects of *opera seria*. Everybody knows 'Where'er you walk'; few know the very funny dialogue between Juno and Somnus. In any case, we assembled a company of soloists, chorus, small orchestra and dancers (one of whom, Mimi Kenny, became my wife in 1957). Looking back, sixty years later, I find that my 'Assistant Conductor' was David Cairns. Among the soloists were Maureen Lehane, Thetis Blacker (who was to sing Mother Goose in *The Rake's Progress* at Glyndebourne in 1975) and Walter Todds, whose contribution to BBC TV's arts programmes was to be very distinguished.

We performed in the Chanticleer Theatre, part of the Webber Douglas School, and whether we were good, bad or indifferent I have no idea, but I suspect we were not *very* good. Certainly we worked from a no doubt corrupt Novello edition. After all, 'authentic' performance was years in the future. So it pleased me when, not long ago, Covent Garden, in their programme for a Handel production, cited our *Semele* as a pioneering effort. Even more gratifying was the discovery that, in the Handel archive in Halle, where the composer was born, we were recorded and named.

But after *Semele* there was a long hiatus. I had been doing some rather unrewarding voluntary work at the British Museum, when I read of the opening of the Handel House Museum in November 2001. Volunteers were sought and were invited to apply, naming two 'referees'. I thought this odd – but obliged: my sponsors were Tom Hemsley and Mickie Rose, who, though he had been our repetiteur for *Semele*, nearly fifty years before, was not a Handel specialist. But, between them, Tom and Mickie secured my acceptance as a bona fide, photo-identification-bearing volunteer at the Museum. The work turned out to be agreeable, my colleagues very congenial: they included retired head teachers, a solicitor or two, a structural engineer and several whose professional background remained obscure and who I liked to think may have been spies. We were often joined by 'interns', mostly female, young and pretty, often Italian or American, sometimes black, who enlivened our proceedings in a welcome way. Museum visitors ranged from boring and bored (why *did* they come?) to intelligent and stimulating. They came from literally all over the world: mainland China *and* Taiwan, Russia, Latin America, Japan (often with no English at all, but obsequiously smiling good manners) – and, of course, Germany, with whom it was never a problem to reach a genial understanding that, though Handel was born a German, he became a naturalised Englishman who spent most of his creative life in London. Establishing a rapport with all these people was not always easy: one had to gather intuitively what kind of approach they might welcome. Some clearly liked oral introduction and explanation. Others, equally clearly, preferred to read the available information and to look at the exhibits at their own quiet pace. When a group appeared with children it was important to talk at a simple level, but without condescension. Sometimes it became obvious that the visitor was well informed, perhaps a professional musician, so that conversational exchange became relaxed and natural. Some visitors soon made it clear that they believed they knew more than you did: these it was best forbearingly to indulge. Once I was offered a tip by a charming, elderly Swede.

In the spring of 2013 I gave a short talk in what had been Handel's rehearsal room. Here is a slightly shortened version of what I said:

Handel's father, a barber-surgeon, "strictly forbad him to meddle with any musical instrument", but the boy managed to smuggle a clavichord into the attic, where he practised so assiduously that, at 17, he was appointed organist of the Domkirche at Halle, where the family lived and where he had been born.

At 18 he went to Hamburg and joined the Opera orchestra as a violinist. He got to know Johann Mattheson (with whom he later fought a duel over the question of which of them should play the harpsichord in a performance of Mattheson's opera *Cleopatra*) and they travelled together to Lübeck, where there was a vacancy for organist in succession to Buxtehude. Unfortunately, a condition of the appointment was marriage to Buxtehude's daughter, who was evidently no beauty.

Handel's first biographer said that "his Amours were rather of short duration". But it seems likely that in Rome in 1707 he had an affair with Margherita Durastanti, a singer for whom he composed cantatas, though she had "a jutting chin and large breasts".

Of Handel's own appearance Sir John Hawkins said "he was ... a large made and very portly man. His gait ... was rather ungraceful." Dr Burney thought "his look was somewhat heavy and sour, but when he did smile, it was ... the sun bursting out of a black cloud."

We know *exactly* what his face was like; a life-mask exists. Thomas Hudson painted him more than once and there are at least three busts by Roubiliac. There is also a charming, informal painting by Mercier: Handel wears a red house-hat, but no cravat. He is leaning on a harpsichord and I like to think it was painted in this room. There is not much doubt that it was out of one of these windows that he threatened to throw the temperamental Cuzzoni.

147

He could be fierce, but he was witty. When a singer called Gordon lost his temper and threatened to jump on Handel's harpsichord, he replied, "Let me know when you will do that and I will advertise it – for ... more people would come to see you jump than hear you sing."

Of his own *Theodora* he said, "the Jews will not come to it because it is a Christian story, and the Ladies will not come because it is a virtuous one."

And, walking in Pleasure Gardens near here, he asked his companion what he thought of the music the band was playing. "Very poor stuff," came the reply. "You are right," said Handel, "I thought so myself when I had finished it."

In 1737 Handel was "struck with the palsy, which took away the use of four fingers in his right hand." So he visited the vapour-baths at Aachen where "...his sweats were profuse beyond what can well be imagined". And he was cured, very soon playing the organ again.

But by 1754 he was blind. He was treated by a quack named Taylor (who also treated Bach) and by a Dr Sharp from Guy's Hospital. To no avail. However, he continued to compose with the help of an amanuensis, John Christopher Smith, and to conduct from the keyboard, notably his annual *Messiah* at the Foundling Hospital, of which he was a founding father – as he was of the Fund for Decayed Musicians, now the Royal Society of Musicians.

The early months of 1759 were exceptionally strenuous and after a performance of *Messiah* on 6 April he went home to this house and took to his bed, dying – upstairs – at about 8 a.m. on 14 April, Holy Saturday. He was buried in Westminster Abbey six days later.

Handel's estate was valued at about £20,000. He left £1000 to the Fund for Decayed Musicians and a fair copy of *Messiah* to the Foundling Hospital. *All* of his music he left to John Christopher Smith the elder. (The younger Smith, who inherited it in 1763, presented it to the Royal Library and there it stayed till our present Queen, in the 1950s, gave it to what is now the British Library.) After various personal bequests – he remembered all his servants – what was left went to his niece, Johanna Floerken, in Germany.

Handel was in every sense a good man. He walked to St George's, Hanover Square, on Sunday mornings. And he kept up with old friends, sending Telemann some "exotic plants" nearly fifty years after they first met.

In Italy he was known as '*il caro Sassone*' – the dear Saxon. And though he was German (if naturalised in 1727) he set many Italian texts. So it is perhaps not too fanciful to think of him as '*il caro Inglese*'.

# 21

## Cumbria 2 – Cragg Cottage and Haile Hall

Not long after my acquisition of Cragg Cottage, I drove over to Haile Hall, where Mollie Ponsonby, my kinswoman, lived. As the crow flies, the house is about five miles away, but by road round the hills, nearer thirty. Sometimes known as 'the cradle of the family', the house became a Ponsonby home in about 1300 and over the years it was extended rather haphazardly. In the mid-seventeenth century a Captain John Ponsonby was the owner and most of his progeny moved to Ireland, where they flourished and became grandees – Bessborough, Sysonby, de Mauley. Some stayed behind and were not ennobled. I am one of those.

Mollie, Lady Ponsonby, had married Sir John in 1935. He had served in the Coldstream Guards and had retired with the rank of Major-General, despite the fact that he had a cleft palate and was hard to understand. By all accounts his soldiers adored him. He was very brave, very amusing and admirably eccentric: he had an aversion to tin hats, so had a hat made out of cardboard, properly covered with hessian but very lightweight so that, during a tour of inspection in the front lines of the 1914–18 war, it blew off and away towards the Germans.

In 1929 Sir John published *The Ponsonby Family*, a very carefully researched record of family history and relationships. At about the same time he bought back into the family Haile Hall, which had been vacant for several years and, with Mollie, he planted gloriously profuse rhododendrons and azaleas

150

around the entrance to the house. He died in 1952 and Mollie's widowhood was to last for just over fifty years. There was no child.

I called on Mollie regularly and always found her buoyant and amusing. As she aged she suffered small afflictions and sometimes went to hospital. After one such visit she told me she had said to her nurse, "Nurse, there's going to be a fatality in this hospital quite soon and it's going to be me: I am *dying* of hunger." On another occasion she told me she had had a call from Ashley Ponsonby, a relative who lived in the South and who had said, "Mollie dear, there are two South African Ponsonbys who would very much like to visit Haile Hall and to meet you. Could you possibly entertain them?" "So I said, 'Of course, Ashley.' Then he said, 'They're black.' I wondered what my John would have done and I decided he would have welcomed them. So I did – and they came – and they were very nice."

On one of my visits Mollie showed me some large watercolours of Windsor Castle. They were, she said, the work of John's mother, Lady (Mary) Ponsonby, whose husband, Henry, had been Queen Victoria's private secretary for twenty-five years. They had lived in Windsor Castle and the watercolours were, Mollie told me, copies of the Queen's collection of Paul Sandby's drawings. I looked at them and found them of 'good amateur' standard. But one of them was obviously professional and in sparkling condition: it *had* to be by Sandby himself. I told Mollie and asked her, half-jokingly, to let me have first refusal if she decided to sell it. But in due course Sotheby's were involved and the drawing was featured on the cover of a catalogue of fine English watercolours. It fetched £130,000, but we do not know whether the Queen was the buyer. As to how it came to be at Haile Hall, I have enjoyed speculating about two alternative scenarios, the first –

Lady P.: Ma'am, I wonder if I might borrow one more of your Sandby watercolours. I have so much enjoyed copying them.

Queen V.: By all means, my dear – and why don't you keep one of them as a souvenir.

In the other scenario, the Queen makes no such suggestion – and the watercolour is not returned to the Royal Collection, no doubt inadvertently!

Mollie's 100th birthday, on 3 July 2001, was celebrated at Haile Hall by neighbours and relations. She was in good form, if rather immobile. But not long afterwards she moved to a care home down the coast at Kirksanton where I once visited her. I found her asleep on a chaise longue and, uncertain what to do, I gently squeezed her wrist. She woke very slowly and murmured, "John?" I haven't the smallest doubt that her memory had wafted her back to the days when her husband – "my John" – was still alive. She died not very long afterwards.

Originally, Haile Hall was to be left to Tom Ponsonby, Opposition Chief Whip in the House of Lords from 1982 to 1990 and a popular figure, energetic and cultivated. Unhappily, he pre-deceased Mollie and, disconcerted by this accident, she decided to leave the house to her niece, Virginia Phipps, who passed it to her daughter, Elizabeth. 'Wiz', her nickname, seemed the ideal proprietor: she loved the place, had energy – and some money. For a while all went very well. The roof was made watertight, dry rot was eliminated. In the garden – large, wild and irregular – some modest landscaping took place and in an adjacent field potatoes were grown. There were pigs – and excellent sausages. Wiz seemed inexhaustible.

But something went wrong and relations and kinsfolk learned, almost by accident, that Haile Hall and its contents were to be sold, variously – at Sotheby's, in Edinburgh and in Cockermouth, the local market town.

So after eight centuries, Haile Hall passed out of Ponsonby hands.

* * * * *

At a very late stage, Haile Hall was bought by an Irish kinsman, Tristan Ponsonby, of Kilcooley.

# 22

## Hindsight – professional

Writing in Cragg Cottage on a still June day in 2015, I am amazed by two things. First, that I am still 'around' (as the weather is, the forecasters repeatedly tell us). Second, that my professional career was advanced at almost every stage by the greatest good luck. When I knocked on Glyndebourne's door in 1950 I had nothing to offer except (amateur) operatic activity at Oxford. But the job I was given was a new one – so perhaps a novice could do it. Then, within the Glyndebourne/Edinburgh family in the Baker Street office, it made sense for me to join the Edinburgh Festival staff as Ian Hunter's assistant. When Ian left the Festival I can only suppose that the appointments committee decided that a young man they knew, who presumably knew the ropes and who was not likely to be troublesome, was preferable to a possibly awkward outsider, however experienced and grand.

After Edinburgh, the Bahamian job fell into my lap and my appointment with the Independent Television Authority was the consequence, I was later told, of my having written a letter to *The Times* praising the programmes of the ITV companies and comparing them favourably with those of their American equivalents. As to the Scottish National Orchestra, I have little doubt that it was Alex Gibson who urged his Board to appoint me.

In no single case was the post advertised. But if there was no published advertisement for the BBC appointment – Controller, Music – discreet letters from Ian Trethowan were sent to a number of 'possibles', suggesting that they might be interested in succeeding William Glock. This seemed to me then, and seems to me now, a good way of proceeding: the BBC knew what kind of person they were looking for and where they were likely to find him (or her). The other day, though, they thought fit to hire a head-hunter (a profession Hans Keller would certainly have described as 'bogus') when looking for a successor to Roger Wright as Director of the Proms. One applicant, a well-regarded instrumental soloist of known eclectic tastes with experience of running a serious music festival, was seen by this person and the following exchange took place:

Head-hunter: You would need to remember that the BBC has four symphony orchestras.

Applicant: I wouldn't need reminding: I have played concertos with all of them.

(I cannot vouch that this account is verbatim, but it came from the applicant's agent and is essentially accurate.) The applicant was not interviewed.

It sometimes seems as if the BBC's wounds are self-inflicted. When John Birt was appointed Director-General and imposed measures which were supposed to be hyper-efficient, one of them – the 'internal market' – had the unexpected, and surely ridiculous, consequence that music producers sometimes found that what they needed – music, recordings, whatever – was cheaper in the Tottenham Court Road than within the BBC. And Birt-speak persists, if *Private Eye* is anything to go by, which I have generally found it is. Erstwhile colleagues tell me they call it "bureau-crap": *mot juste*.

But of course the BBC's present malaise cannot be ascribed to John Birt alone; nor to the Jimmy Savile scandal, nor even to the Newsnight fiasco. Perhaps to the mediocrity of many television programmes (too much over-acted cooking, too many seriously over-acted auctions, too many money-motivated quizzes)? Who knows? What is obvious is the absence of clear statements about policy and character – for example, what clearly distinguishes BBC2 from BBC1? Lord (Tony) Hall has yet to show his hand – but it needs to be a strong one for the future governance and funding of the corporation are seriously at issue. Where music is concerned, the symphony orchestras (all very good at the moment), the excellent BBC Singers (though already slightly reduced in numbers) and, above all, the Proms are likely to survive any harsh economies called for by negotiation of the charter: they are the BBC's cultural credentials. And Radio 3, though its presentation is chaotic and it is shy of serious talk about music, remains a uniquely enjoyable – sometimes inspiring – and, in the best sense of the word, educative force.

# 23

## Hindsight - personal

To fly from Hong Kong to Melbourne, as I did early in 1982, was awe-inspiring: the Australian continent seemed immeasurably vast and the landscape below quite empty. But I was on BBC business, the Symphony Orchestra on tour, and similar visits took me to Moscow, Tokyo, Beijing and Shanghai, all of them fleetingly and frustratingly short.

Much more rewarding and enjoyable were holidays – mostly in and around the Mediterranean. The first two were conventional undergraduate expeditions. In 1948, in a pre-war Austin 10, Robert Goff and I drove to the south of France, doing scant justice, en route, to Beauvais, Fontainebleau and Avignon, but marvelling at Viollet-le-Duc's toy-town restoration of Carcassonne and, infinitely more impressive, the architectural miracle of the Pont du Gard. On our last day, feeling enjoyably naughty, we attended the Folies Bergères. Had we been a year or two earlier we would have heard, unwittingly, Pierre Boulez manipulating the *ondes martenot*, his first paid employment. Indeed, at about that time he wrote a Quartet for four *ondes*, whose synthetic wailing in quadruplicate beggars imagination. He was wise to withdraw it. Only Messiaen, whom Boulez admired as a man, but not as a composer, has, I think, used the instrument persuasively.

No *ondes* flavoured the music I heard in Italy the following year. With two Trinity friends (one, Richard Incledon, to become a Roman Catholic priest) I travelled by train to Florence where, in seven breathless days we saw, or at least glimpsed, all the 'unmissable' glories of that noisy city which, because it sits in a saucer surrounded by hills, is seriously exhausting. Nevertheless, a first encounter with both Michelangelo and Botticelli had to be momentous, as had the discovery of Donatello, whose bronze David is to my mind much more touching than Michelangelo's massive marble. We heard no music in Florence, but a few days in Rome yielded my first *Tosca*. The cast was excellent, Maria Caniglia the Tosca, Ferruccio Tagliavini Cavaradossi and Paolo Silveri Scarpia. But the performance was in the Baths of Caracalla, a vast open-air arena in which the singers were so remote as to resemble puppets and the audience (nearly all of whom seemed to be enjoying 'gelati' or 'cioccolati') so amiably restless that the occasion was more social than musical: for one thing no *fortissimo* was possible, and *pianissimos* tended to be inaudible. A few days later, Donizetti's *Lucia di Lammermoor* made little impression: the singers were uninteresting but the chorus, the men in Italianate kilts with sporrans skew-whiff, irresistibly funny.

Between *Tosca* and *Lucia* I heard Josef Krips conducting Beethoven's 'Choral' Symphony in the Basilica di Massenzio, another open-air auditorium. The performance sounded good, if rather low-powered, but the evening was made enjoyable by my immediate neighbour, a rotund man in early middle age who was determined to talk – about music and musicians. His English was even more primitive than my Italian, but we managed quite well trilingually, also making use of French. He asked me whether Krips was our English "primo direttore" and I realised that he was muddling Josef Krips with Sir Stafford Cripps. But he was right about John Barbirolli, whose father was Venetian. When Venice produces an artist, he said, "elle produit un vrai artiste. Moi, je suis Vénitien!" He asked me if perhaps Gigli was "trop pleureux pour les Anglais" and expressed boundless admiration for Toscanini. He specially amused me by describing Cortot as "ce vieux effigie". In any case, because I had arrived early and the concert started very late, he was an entertaining companion whom it was easy to forgive when he vigorously 'conducted' the most obviously rhythmic passages in the symphony's last movement.

Before setting out for England, we of course visited the Sistine Chapel and, outside Rome, Tivoli and the Villa d'Este, with its echoes of Liszt. In the Catacombs we were shown a moving statue of St Cecilia, patron saint of music, whose martyrdom was by all accounts exceptionally painful. Finally, after a morning in and around the Forum, we made what turned out to be a very unwise decision: we would hitch-hike northwards. So, on a very hot day in mid-July, after fifteen hours on six different vehicles, we arrived at Livorno, barely 100 miles north of Rome. Next day was much worse. We reached Viareggio, via Pisa (not even glimpsed), after more than twelve miles on foot. Burned and blistered, we surrendered. The bus to Genoa passed Rapallo (no time to visit Max Beerbohm, subtlest of satirists) and at Genoa we took the train to the French frontier at Ventimiglia – and so, by rail, to Paris and London.

Salzburg and Yugoslavia were my next two holiday destinations: both are touched on elsewhere in this book. But Sicily, in 1953, gave me one of the most evocative images of my whole life. With Michael Willis-Fleming, an erstwhile brother-officer, I sailed from Naples through the Lipari Islands at dawn to Palermo, a city we had decided not to loiter in. (I was lucky, though, by chance to see some of the work of Serpotta, Sicily's Grinling Gibbons. In one of his set pieces among the fluttering *putti* I happened to spot one who remained airborne by holding on to the private parts of the one above.) Moving south, we saw the glittering mosaics of the Cathedral of Monreale, a Norman church much more remarkable than any in Palermo. But it was the Greek temples we had come to see and the nearest was the temple of Hera at Segesta. Standing alone among the hills, it is uniquely imposing – and Michael and I had it to ourselves until there trotted by a shaggy pony, its rider a peasant boy. Wearing only coarse breeches and riding bare-back he was swarthy but not hirsute except for a head of black curls. He was no Adonis – more a young Bacchus, for in his left hand (his right gripped a rough halter) he held above his upturned face a bunch of white grapes which he bit into, the juice running down his chest. He was elementally a part of the Sicilian landscape – and I have never seen a more beautiful human being. I suppose that I photographed him, but my camera was cleverly stolen in Rome station a week or so later (along with everything except what I stood up in). Perhaps it was as well: imagination is preferable to cold black-and-white precision.

Corsica, which I visited in 1954, was, culturally, a far cry from Sicily: no fine architecture to speak of, only one modestly important gallery, the Musée Fesch. But the mountainous scenery, sharply vertical like the Dolomites, the rocky coastline and the scent of arbutus and other fragrant herbs – the *maquis* – I found uniquely pleasant. I concentrated upon the west coast not only for its scenery but also for Napoleon's birthplace in Ajaccio, a substantial building in a quiet square where his family had lived for many years. Calvi, further north, has surely been established as the birthplace of Christopher Columbus by Joseph Chiari in his authoritative book, *Corsica: Columbus's Isle* (in which a handful of my photos appear and in which Jo, French consul in Edinburgh when I knew him, states that the photographer "knows Corsica well"!). After Calvi and Ajaccio I went south to Bonifacio, one day walking to the tip of the island, picking figs as I went and, within easy sight of Sardinia (which I visited in 1956), went skinny-dipping on a small idyllic beach, the only passer-by an unsurprised goatherd.

Jo's book was not yet published, but I had been lent a copy of Edward Lear's *Journal of a Landscape Painter in Corsica* and this admirable diary, in places very funny, had the unexpected effect not just of illuminating Corsica but of igniting in me a lifelong love of Lear the artist and Lear the man. From time to time I have owned various works of his but here I will refer to only two, neither of them 'important'. The first – my earliest acquisition – was (I still have it) a tiny watercolour of Cape Sunium in Greece, all pale blues with a soft sepia outline and a characteristically precise inscription: "1864. Sunium. 6 April. 4pm." (That year he had already been to Corfu and was to go to Crete.) For this small treasure Agnew's charged me four guineas in 1956. What I paid for my other Lear I don't remember. It was a pencil drawing of Hastings Church from the downs above. Lear was there in 1852, but he did not date the drawing. Instead there was an inscription, "Oh man, please do say it again", and I haven't the smallest doubt about what happened. As Lear sat drawing, a child approached him and they talked, Lear (who was perfectly in tune with childhood) at one point saying something funny, the child's request in turn amusing Lear, who wrote it down. Sixteen years earlier, in 1836, he had been in the Lake District, once walking over Honister Pass from Borrowdale into Buttermere valley and on through Buttermere village, necessarily passing close to Cragg Cottage en route to Ennerdale. At some point he stopped and made a drawing of Fleetwith Pike and Haystacks. He cannot have been far from the spot at which Turner made a sketch for his big, dark oil of Fleetwith. But as watercolourists the two painters differed utterly: there was no trace of impressionism in Lear – instead a luminous clarity, broad washes of colour within elegant lines – as Francis Towne before and D.Y. Cameron after him demonstrated. He was immensely prolific, bringing back 350 drawings from his Corsican visit alone. He occasionally

161

painted in oils, but these were not successful, being too busy, too fussy. The watercolours – and of course the parrots and toucan prints for Gould – are his glories, but his songs – settings of Tennyson – are best glossed over: they are amateurish and primly Victorian, his vamping at the piano said to have been embarrassing.

Lear's childlike innocence must have been attractive. But he was tough: his epilepsy notwithstanding, he walked great distances and was an intrepid traveller. Once stoned in Albania by hostile locals, he suffered many other less violent hardships, sometimes recording them in drawings which remind me by their nursery absurdity of those by James Thurber.

Another amateur pianist – and a much better one – was E.M. Forster, whose work (if not quite all of it) I greatly admire. In his essays on music in the wonderful collection *Two Cheers for Democracy*, he writes with amazing perception about the nature and colour of particular keys and about his preference for abstract over programmatic music. About his own playing he makes "an important point: my own performances upon the piano. These grow worse yearly, but never will I give them up. For one thing, they compel me to attend [...] For another thing, they teach me a little about construction [...] Playing Beethoven, as I generally do, I grow familiar with his tricks, his impatience, his sudden softnesses, his dropping of a tragic theme one semitone, his love, when tragic, for the key of C minor [...] This gives me a physical approach to Beethoven which cannot be gained through the slough of 'appreciation'. Even when people play as badly as I do, they should continue: it will help them to listen."

I once met Forster – in the Nag's Head before a performance of Strauss's *Salome* at Covent Garden. He was alone and I introduced myself (I hope not too gushingly) as an admirer. He was friendly and talkative, at one point saying, "The trouble with *Salome* is that Oscar Wilde was such a goose." I didn't know then, and I don't know now, what he meant – but the remark went straight into my Commonplace Book. His best-known remark, though, comes in his essay, 'What I Believe': "[...] if I had to choose between betraying my country and betraying my friend, I hope I should have the guts to betray my country." That is admirable, but I find more attractive, because it immediately rang for me a resonant bell, his statement that, "I believe in aristocracy [...] an aristocracy of the sensitive, the considerate and the plucky" (a very Forsterian word). Self-evidently he belonged to this elite himself, as did Lear – perhaps an even more distinguished member. They also had India in common: Lear was there in 1873–4; Forster served as secretary and adviser to the Maharajah of Dewas in 1921–2, an experience which sparked his masterpiece, *A Passage to India*. But Lear's Indian watercolours are not, I think, among his very best.

Wherever he was, Lear generally annotated his drawings, as did one of his forerunners, William Crotch, professionally a musician, but also a good amateur watercolourist. Crotch was an interesting man: a child prodigy on organ and harpsichord, he became a prolific composer mainly of church music (his oratorio *Palestine* was revived by Jonathan Rennert in 1973). He knew Constable and in 1812 (when he was 37) the two put on a puppet performance of *Henry V*, Constable painting one of the sets. In the Norfolk Record Office there is a pencil sketch by Constable of 'W Crotch playing Mozart'. The composer's zenith came in 1822 when he was appointed Principal of the newly created Royal Academy of Music, a post he held until 1831 when, apparently, he was caught kissing one of his students and was forced to resign. He must have been a likeable man, his drawings perhaps more interesting than his music. I have owned a number of them, the most attractive a church interior inscribed, "Surrey: [Interior of] Gatton Church. August 1835. While drawing this I was hearing Bach and

163

Handel on a fine organ", a drawing which I gave to the Royal Academy of Music to add to their own collection.

Long before his appointment to the Royal Academy, Crotch had succeeded Philip Hayes as Professor of Music in Oxford University at the age of 21. In 1791, five years earlier, he had heard Haydn directing one of his 'Salomon' symphonies in London and when the impresario brought the great composer to Oxford to receive his Doctorate Crotch played to him in Christ Church Cathedral. But when I went up to Oxford in 1948 I had never heard of Crotch, though I had begun to read Forster. My academic studies did not extend into the twentieth century, so I discovered for myself – it wasn't difficult – the two great Roman Catholic novelists, Waugh and Greene, Waugh's *Sword of Honour* trilogy surely his masterpiece. Of course I laughed at the early social satires (who could not?) but I have always been particularly fond of *Scott-King's Modern Europe*. I think it must owe some of its ideas to Rose Macaulay's *The Towers of Trebizond*, whose first line, "'Take my camel, dear,' said my Aunt Dot" is an irresistible invitation to read the rest of the book which, though sometimes rather heavy on Anglicanism, is original and very entertaining. But another book in at least one sense towers over both Waugh and Greene. Anthony Powell's *A Dance to the Music of Time* comprises twelve novels loosely organised in four groups of three books, all narrated in the first person by Nicholas Jenkins and, flashbacks included, covering about sixty years up to 1970. It is in part a loose *roman-à-clef*, Auden and Isherwood appearing as Parsnip and Pimpernell, Constant Lambert as Hugh Moreland, the sole musician among the innumerable cast (though there is a cello-playing General). The most memorable character is Kenneth Widmerpool, a personality somewhere between Malvolio and King Lear and a strikingly original creation. Powell's control of his characters and their development is masterly. There are a few loose ends, but they are very few and not very loose.

At one point, Nicholas Jenkins says that, "To talk at all objectively about one's own marriage is impossible." And I agree. Nevertheless...

I had met Mimi Kenny in 1954 when she was a dancer in Handel's *Semele*. We married in 1957 on Holy Innocents' Day (a date which, in retrospect, looks peculiarly apt). The wedding was in a Roman Catholic church because she was devoted to her faith and, though I was at the time a communicant Anglican, I was in the eyes of Rome a heretic and we were allowed no music. I had had to take 'instruction' and to promise that children, if any, would be brought up as Roman Catholics. Of course this rankled and though I did my best to suppress such feelings they were, I fear, at the heart of the marriage's deterioration and collapse. Our divorce came through in the autumn of 1969 and I moved out of our rather grand, but rather gloomy, flat in Glasgow's Great Western Terrace, one of the architect 'Greek' Thomson's finest domestic buildings and one in which Sir William Burrell – he of the Burrell Collection – had also had a home. Kirklee Circus, to which I moved, was not far away; it was sunnier and much more *simpatico*.

I suppose I first met Lesley Black after a concert in Glasgow's City Hall: several members of the (Scottish National) Orchestra had been, as she had been, students of the Royal Scottish Academy of Music and she came regularly to the Orchestra's concerts. She was unmissable, having hair which was absolutely not red, but golden. Acquaintance warmed into love and she joined me when I took up my BBC work in 1972. Our first home was in Elsworthy Road – just north of Primrose Hill – a few doors along from a house in which Henry Wood had lived. But in 1974 we moved to a big flat (with room for a grand piano) in Ornan Road, half a mile

165

south of Hampstead Heath, on land apparently once owned by Arnold Bax. We drove north to Cumbria as often as possible – which wasn't often, the BBC's demands too taxing – taking with us not dachshunds but, initially, a single cat and, later, two. We married, in Cockermouth (friendliest of towns), in 1977. There were no problems of religious contention: Lesley was, if anything, a Presbyterian; I was on my way to becoming – what I am today if such a position is possible – an Anglican agnostic. But after a while Lesley's love for me petered out and at the end of 1985 she moved out of my life at the very moment that I left the BBC. For a while I found myself mired in a Slough of Despond, the deepest of my whole life.

# 24

## Mount Pleasant

Not quite Bunyan's Delectable Mountains, Mount Pleasant is a big 1920s house in a big informal garden under the North Downs on the outskirts of Reigate, the birthplace, incidentally, of Margot Fonteyn and the burial-place of Samuel Palmer, whose Shoreham watercolours are one of the finest small glories of English painting. Richly endowed by Francis William Reckitt – Reckitt's mustard and Reckitt's Blue – the house, with just seven bedrooms, was to serve as an 'Artists' Rest Home' and I was introduced to it by Gavin Henderson and Bryan Magee. Gavin, a Brighton-based trumpet player who was to manage the Philharmonia Orchestra, to run the Dartington Summer School, Trinity College of Music and, latterly, to direct the Royal Central School of Speech and Drama, was an able administrator and a convivial colleague whose bursts of whinnying laughter were irresistibly infectious.

Bryan Magee did not laugh so easily: his colossal intellect perhaps weighed too heavily upon him. For a while a Labour MP, he became a popular broadcaster about philosophy on radio and television, he was a novelist and a published poet. At one point he studied music and his little book, *Aspects of Wagner*, is admirable.

Visiting Mount Pleasant for the first time in 1986 I found that the majority of my fellow guests were writers. But among the 'regulars' was the potter Emmanuel Cooper, a world authority on ceramics and a very likeable man, though I did not care for the texture or colouring of his own pots. Bryan Magee was himself the most frequent visitor, industriously writing his many books in long-hand and tending to dominate the conversation at meal-times

167

– a habit which earned him, behind his back, the nickname Wotan. Another prolific writer was Michael Bloch, biographer of Jeremy Thorpe (whom I had known at Eton) and of James Lees-Milne, a pillar of the National Trust, which he advised on the acquisition (or not) of historic country houses. Other subjects of Michael's were Ribbentrop and the Windsors. An engaging conversationalist, he sometimes wore his homosexuality rather too obtrusively on his sleeve: his latest infatuation was not always of much interest to other writers. And his book *Closet Queens* strikes me as gratuitous and ill-advised. But I always enjoyed my visits to Mount Pleasant, particularly when David Cairns, busy with his great book on Berlioz, coincided with me there. Another visitor was John Amis, for whom music was the be-all and end-all of life. An amusing speaker, his script for the sketch 'Punkt Contrapunkt' – part of Gerard Hoffnung's dottily inspired "Interplanetary Music Festival" of 1958 – in which two German musicologists (John and Gerard) discuss and explain a work by the modernist Hans (Henze) Bruno (Maderna) Jaja (Nono) is hilariously full of knowledgeable in-jokes. John could also act impulsively, once calling to say, "Robert, a funny thing's happened: I've been asked to write your obituary." His announcement was apropos because, not long before, John Higgins, in charge of obituaries at *The Times*, had asked me to write a 'stock' obituary of Ian Hunter. By 'stock' was meant 'in advance' of the subject's death – but ready for it. To prevent any embarrassing accident *The Times*'s typescript was pointedly headed NOT UNTIL. I thought it important not to let one's 'victim' know that one was writing his (or her) obituary, so I duly gave John a ripe raspberry, necessarily unable to tell him that I had already written his. My piece for Ian was liked both by John Higgins and, as it turned out, by Ian's family, one of his daughters, Kitty, asking whether – *Times* obituaries being anonymous – they might be allowed to know the name of the obituarist. John consulted me and, having not the smallest objection – on the contrary – I said "yes" and was pleased and touched by Ian's family's approval.

The success of this one obituary led on to many other commissions, a majority from *The Times*, many from the *Independent*, several from the *Guardian*. (A number, including Ian Hunter's, are reproduced in my *Musical Heroes*.) I would not accept such a commission unless I felt I could shed some personal, preferably anecdotal, light upon my 'victim'. A good obituary should convey more than a chronological record of events.

Mount Pleasant was wonderfully conducive to quiet, steady work. There was no obligation to fraternise with other guests; indeed meal-times (when one was expected to be punctual) were the only occasions when such encounters necessarily occurred. Almost always there were interesting people in the house, though I do remember once being one of only three guests, one very deaf, the other very boring. But it was often by no means full and, around 2012, the Trustees, after much heart-searching, came to the conclusion that they had no alternative but to close and sell the house (which was thought to be worth around £3 million), using income from the invested capital to support visits to some other similar establishment. Among the possibilities investigated was Leith Hill Place (not far away on the Downs), which Vaughan Williams had inherited, but never occupied, and which was now a National Trust property. In the end an arrangement was reached (in 2015 still to be activated) with Hawkwood College, near Stroud in Gloucestershire, where pictures – including an Orpen portrait of Reckitt – and inscribed books relating to Mount Pleasant could be suitably preserved. Whether Hawkwood provides the same quiet, collegiate atmosphere as Mount Pleasant remains to be seen.

# 25

## Passing Pleasures

This book is mostly about music and the musicians who have been at the heart of my life. But my work at Edinburgh also encompassed theatre and the visual arts. Georges Braque, whom I visited in Paris in the spring of 1956 and whom I have admired ever since, was remote from my lifelong interest in English watercolours. There was, however, room for both in the picture gallery of my tastes, as there was for two living Scottish painters, Anne Redpath (whom I once encountered in Corsica and from whom I bought a Corsican landscape) and David Donaldson, a painter of unusual vitality and great range. His sitters included the Queen, his subjects Susanna and the Elders, a small version of which I briefly owned and enjoyed. One of his pictures seems to me remarkable. Entitled *Rage* (at the transient nature of beauty) it looks big and empty, but in the centre a nude boy is dragging a white goose away from the viewer, while in the foreground the single stem of a lily is beginning to droop. The scene is hauntingly evocative.

Pictures should make one think (if only, as in Renoir, of pretty women) and perhaps the greatest of all puzzle pictures, Velázquez's *Las Meninas*, I saw in the spring of 1985. I went early to the Prado and, astonishingly, I had the painting entirely to myself for at least ten minutes; I am fascinated by it to this day (though I love more the tender *Old Woman Frying Eggs* in Scotland's National Gallery). A similar experience – but a musical one, this time in Barcelona several years later – was unforgettable. I had gone to see not Gaudí (whom I can do without) but the medieval quarter and there, in the Plaça del Rei – a dark, quiet square – I happened upon a young man sitting on stone steps playing the guitar. He and I were alone in the echoing space for several minutes until some new listeners broke the spell: I felt as poor, mad Ludwig II of Bavaria must have felt when the *lèse-majesté* of intruders disrupted his solitary listening. My young guitarist, though no Segovia nor Bream, was good and naturally easy in the Spanish music he was playing, so that I later reflected that, because of the setting, I would have preferred to hear him again – and for longer – than a famous performer in the cheek-by-jowl discomfort (no leg room) of a crowded Wigmore Hall, its art nouveau decor notwithstanding.

In other words, what you see may enhance what you hear, whether Frederick Ashton's *Symphonic Variations* or a lone piper in a Scottish glen.

I have always enjoyed looking at pictures and I remember, when young, my excitement at the prospect of "going to the pictures" – the cinema. *Hellzapoppin'*, a dotty fantasy, was an early favourite. Then came more serious films: Orson Welles's *Citizen Kane*, of course, and French cinema – Jean Renoir's moody melodramas and Marcel Carné's *Les Enfants du Paradis*, made in Paris with the very beautiful Arletty, who co-starred (if that is the word) with Jean-Louis Barrault. The film was produced in 1944, a year after Pierre Boulez's arrival in Paris. Four years later Barrault appointed him music director of the Théâtre Marigny and the company came to Edinburgh in 1948, its repertoire including *Baptiste*, a 'pantomime' based upon *Les Enfants du Paradis* in which France's mimic tradition was manifest in Barrault's own performance of the title role and – even more remarkably – the great Marcel Marceau in the role of Arlequin. There was no music in this production and Boulez's only contribution to the visit was to conduct Honegger's suite of incidental music for André Gide's

171

translation of *Hamlet*. Later, Barrault was to write with extraordinary perspicacity about the angry young man under whose fractious exterior he had detected a creative talent of rare integrity.

Once, at an awards ceremony years later, Boulez – in his acceptance speech – referred to Chaplin's *Monsieur Verdoux*, to the moment when, on trial for the murder and incineration of a number of wealthy ladies, the judge points a fierce convicting finger at Verdoux (Chaplin), who looks backwards over his shoulder to see whoever it can be who is being pointed at. Boulez said he had similar feelings – of surprise – about his award (a Fellowship from the British Academy of Songwriters, Composers and Authors).

Chaplin – like Marceau and Barrault, a superb mime – was never more subtly funny, it seems to me, than in *Monsieur Verdoux*, which I saw on 18 February 1948 – and again the next day! The film is in effect a long solo, elegantly underplayed, and Chaplin's backwards fall out of an open window is no pratfall but an immaculately timed choreographic device. One couldn't, of course, do without *The Great Dictator*, Chaplin's Adenoid Hynkel a virtuoso performance, but its companion-plot – the Jewish barber harassed by Nazi storm-troopers – is, despite its comic knockabout, marred by sentimentality and, I fear, Chaplin's own mawkish music.

To compare with Chaplin the Scottish actor Stanley Baxter may seem ridiculous, but I make not the smallest apology for doing so. Baxter twice acted in Tyrone Guthrie's legendary Edinburgh Festival production of *The Thrie Estaites* and later in plays, also directed by Guthrie, by James Bridie and Eric Linklater, none of his roles particularly comic. But his performance as Dr Prentice in Joe Orton's last (and best) farce, *What the Butler Saw*, marked him as having a genius for comedy. It was in the early '70s that he was 'discovered' by television, and his annual Show, transmitted at Christmas time, soon became essential viewing for those in the know. His ear was amazing (his Gielgud uncannily accurate), his face and body infinitely adaptable (anyone from Liza Minelli and Joan Bakewell to the Queen) and his scripts brilliant. He could sing well and dance very well. But apparently the cost of the Show, which called for a band, occasionally a choir, twelve or so good dancers, complicated choreography with lavish sets and costumes, eventually became unaffordable and, because Baxter himself was imperceptibly ageing, it was dropped. Thank goodness that laugh-aloud DVDs are available: he was a satirist and impersonator of genius.

It is said that when Joe Orton first saw Laurence Olivier in action, he said, "This isn't acting; it's impersonation." I know exactly what he meant: when technique becomes obtrusive and spontaneity is lost, then its power to convey emotion is also lost – the viewer suspects a fraud, though the technique may dazzle. And I have seen nothing more dazzling than Olivier's double bill of *Oedipus* and Mr Puff in Sheridan's *The Critic*. But in *Othello* – that most painful of almost all plays (and in Verdi's opera quite unbearable) – everything he did seemed studied and, so, unmoving. His squawking performance in *Richard III* I found unwatchable – and unlistenable.

Driving to Cumbria I often listen to Alec Guinness's recordings of his own diaries. Faultlessly delivered in what I suppose is RP (long may it be preserved!) they are beautifully paced, human and humane. He was of course a comedian of genius, but his range was spectacular, *Tunes of Glory*, in which he plays a red-haired, rasp-voiced Scottish soldier, even more remarkable than *The Bridge on the River Kwai*, and utterly remote from T.S. Eliot's *The Cocktail Party* at Edinburgh in 1949, when he was the 'Unidentified Guest' – an ideally enigmatic role.

My cinema-going has dwindled recently, but I accumulate DVDs, among them *Four Weddings and a Funeral*, which declines with great wit (and splendid casting) from farce to the final funeral, beautifully clouded by Auden's *Funeral Blues* –

> Stop all the clocks, cut off the telephone,
> Prevent the dog from barking with a juicy bone.
> Silence the pianos and with muffled drum
> Bring out the coffin, let the mourners come...

For sheer visual beauty, no film can compare with *Death in Venice*. Visconti stays very close to Mann's novella and he was clearly in love both with the book and with Venice itself. The opening – a smoky steamer approaching over a still sea during a cloudless dawn – is scene-setting of pure magic. And Visconti's mastery of atmosphere persists, whether in the public rooms of Aschenbach's grand hotel on the Lido, or on its uninteresting beach, virtually every scene directly or indirectly dominated by the Polish boy, Tadzio, on holiday with his aristocratic and gloriously costumed family. Aschenbach, who has a wife and child at home in Austria, is bewitched – and fatally. The boy, whose role is mute, is played by Björn Andrésen, himself beguilingly beautiful, and he hits off to perfection a facial response to Aschenbach's reckless adoration which is not quite come-hither, but curious, with a touch of pity. The film is surely one of the masterpieces of cinema, Mahler's music emotionally ideal.

Finally, a great artist – Fred Astaire. It is impossible to imagine that any dancer will ever combine virtuosity with irresistible charm and pinpoint precision in the same degree. He is *hors concours*, and I take off my Top Hat to him and the dancers, actors, painters and writers who have thrilled me or made me laugh.

# 26

## Five Friends

## 1 – Wilfrid Blunt

At the end of my first half* at Eton my drawing report read, "He is improving rapidly."

Signed "WJWB", this non-committal reference is the earliest communication from Wilfrid Blunt that I have kept; it is dated December 1939. The latest is dated December 1984.

There was boundless room for improvement, but in the end it was not drawing that Wilfrid taught me, but a consuming love for all the arts, particularly music. He was, in that context, the ideal role-model (to use a fashionable demographic cliché): singer, painter, writer, poet, traveller, gardener and linguist. He was appointed 'Drawing Master' at Eton in 1938 and was therefore a successor to Alexander Cozens and Robert Hills, among others. The Drawing Schools – then as now – were on the periphery of Eton at the far end of the Parade Ground, where the Officers' Training Corps drilled. They were therefore 'apart' and to visit what was effectively the Drawing Master's private domain induced a small but agreeable thrill. On Sunday evenings Wilfrid regularly invited a handful of senior boys with an interest in music to listen to gramophone records and in this way I heard a range of music which covered four centuries – from Vecchi's *L'Amfiparnaso* to Stravinsky's early ballets. These gatherings were not subversive, but they had a certain glamour and Wilfrid liked to poke fun at the Head

---

* Eton-speak for 'term'

Master, who was not only tone-deaf but apparently thought musicians disreputable. In the second volume of his autobiography, *Slow on the Feather*, Wilfrid describes the experience of a boy he chose to call 'O' (in fact a friend of mine, Oscar Yerburgh, who confirms the truth of what follows). 'Okky', who was a gifted pianist, had decided to make music his profession, but when this was reported to the Head Master by a relative, he said, "I'd sooner have heard that he'd taken to drink." It wasn't quite clear that the remark was ironical.

This deep-dyed philistinism was characteristic of Eton at that time. (Today, all has changed: the Drawing Schools have been extended; there is a superbly equipped new Music School, and it is not uncommon for boys to be ARCO [Associate of the Royal College of Organists].) But there was another subtext: to be 'artistic', let alone an aesthete, was very possibly to be a homosexual and though 'crushes' and sexual horseplay were not uncommon, they were indulged, if at all, with utmost discretion. Now, Wilfrid – though we had no notion of it – was 'gay'. His conduct towards the boys, however, was immaculate and his very amusing but frank memoirs will have come as a shock to some of his colleagues and pupils. Their author was prodigiously talented. In 1935 he had given a Wigmore Hall recital – he was a baritone – comprising lieder by Schubert, Schumann, Brahms, Wolf and Strauss, with songs in Russian, Norwegian and English. It was well received. He was an admirable portrait-painter and I can remember to this day an 'oils' of an Irish girl which I was happy to find reproduced on page 19 of *Slow on the Feather*.

His autobiography apart, he published twenty-four books, of which at least one, *The Art of Botanical Illustration*, is a classic and one which I am happy to have on my shelves, for it is now a rarity. In the field of music, he wrote *John Christie of Glyndebourne*, an amusing study of that great and lovable eccentric, and *On Wings of Song*, a lavishly illustrated (but not specially illuminating) biography of Mendelssohn. Leaving Eton in 1959 Wilfrid was appointed Curator of the Watts Gallery, near Guildford, and *England's Michelangelo*, a study of G.F. Watts published in 1975, was the natural outcome.

It was from the Watts Gallery that he wrote the last letter I had from him:

Every Christmas I get a handful of xeroxed letters from people I scarcely remember, updating their own lives and those of their innumerable children and grandchildren whom I have never met [...] This letter will contain nothing about anybody except ME; if you cannot recall who I am, or do recall but do not care – then read no further. If you are still with me, you will be longing to learn 'in depth' about my state of health. Just another little tidying-up cancer op. in November: nothing to worry about. I don't really enjoy being Cellotaped daily to a mortuary slab. Also I am not allowed to wash my neck for six weeks, and it is gradually assuming the rich *café-au-lait* colour that the French call *isabelle* [...] In addition I am taking folic acid tablets; these were also prescribed for my housekeeper when she was pregnant, but I think this is coincidental. More disabling than my cancers is something mysteriously called R. Thritis, which has reduced me to two sticks and a snail's-crawl.

*Married to a Single Life* has sold so unexpectedly well that I have decided to get the admirable Michael Russell to publish the second volume of my three-tier autobiography, covering my years (1938–1959) at Eton, as soon as possible. It will, I fear, offend everyone – as all *frank* autobiographies must. If, as Harold Nicolson wrote in *Some People*, one pauses to consider what Aunt Juliet might say of one's book in Littlehampton, or Uncle Roderick at Bath, nothing would ever get written. Anyhow, I shall be approaching my eighty-sixth year (or already be dead) by the time it appears. Volume 2 has as yet no title; but if I live to complete the third and final instalment – Compton, and beyond? – it shall be called *Over my Dead Body* and appear posthumously.

And how are you? Oh, I *am* sorry! There's a lot of it around this winter…

[handwritten] With best wishes to you both for Xmas and 1985
Yours ever,
Wilfrid

Wilfrid died in 1987. To his talent, his industry and his candour must certainly be added two further admirable characteristics: humour and courage.

\* \* \* \* \*

# 2 – Roger Toulmin

Twice a refugee, I was taken in by Roger with unhesitating generosity.

On 4 October 1953, travelling back from Sicily by train, I was seriously robbed: everything except what I stood up in was ingeniously taken in Rome's main station and I arrived in Paris, then Roger's home, cold and bereft.

Much more prolonged and onerous was my occupation of his spare room in Elsworthy Terrace, just north of Primrose Hill, for nearly a month in November/December 1985. I was at a low ebb: my last day at the BBC was 29 November and Lesley moved out of our marital home on 27 December. Roger could not have been more solicitous. When he died in 1993 I wrote his obituary for *The Times*. Here it is:

Roger Toulmin had three careers. As a journalist he represented *The Times* in Paris and New Delhi in the 1950s; for a while he provided scripts for the BBC's External Services and the Third Programme; and, latterly, he was a civil servant in the then Department of Health and Social Security. Every phase of his professional life was enhanced by a striking ability to communicate, on paper, with elegant and precise economy. Towards its very end he translated from French a history of the Daughters of Jesus of Kermaria and edited a selection of Gerald Priestland's last writings and talks. He was a natural wordsmith.

Born in Hampstead, Toulmin was educated at Winchester where he converted to Roman Catholicism. He served as a conscript in the Royal Navy before reading History at Magdalen College, Oxford. He had a quite exceptional brain, a capacious memory and a fine ear for European languages. But he had other talents, among them a strong baritone voice and a weighty physical presence. These earned him the role of Benedick in the university opera club's staged performances of Stanford's *Much Ado About Nothing*. He loved music and was dauntingly well read. Though the survivor of a fearful air crash on take-off from New Delhi in 1958, he continued to enjoy travel by air. He was equally happy walking in the Lake District.

Though for a time he did not go to church, he was fundamentally a devout Christian. But he was neither puritan nor prig. Friends will remember him organising a large party for a visit to *Ah! les Belles Bacchantes*, a sophisticated, but witty, Parisian revue. Some of the same friends were present at a fireworks party he gave in a smallish London backyard when a rogue rocket got among those awaiting ignition, setting them prematurely and simultaneously alight. Toulmin's prancing silhouette, dodging the missiles and yelling with gleeful alarm at each near miss, remains unforgettable.

Both a sociable and a solitary man, he would no doubt have liked to marry: he adored and was adored by the children and grandchildren of his brother, Stephen. But some diffidence where commitment was concerned got in his way. And this diffidence, which manifested itself in other spheres, was surely the reason why he was (as a BBC colleague put it) "undervalued" throughout his working life. It is true that he was a man of such fiercely obdurate principle that he could exasperate even those who loved him ("I want you to want to…" was a characteristic phrase). Yet his transparent integrity made him easily forgiveable. Indeed, he positively commanded affection.

Roger Toulmin was blessed with that rare and enviable quality, innocence. Obversely, he was easily wounded. As to courage, his deep Catholic convictions enabled him to face his death with serene clarity of mind and spirit.

He was never famous, nor concerned to be, but if modesty, delicacy, gentleness and solicitude had been the standards of our coarse times he would have been eminent.

\* \* \* \* \*

# 3 – Royd Barker

At a memorial occasion for Royd, on 25 February 2013, I gave this address:

I *think* I first met Royd on 10 March 1949, after a performance in Oxford of George Tolhurst's laughably bathetic *Ruth*: one chorus opens with the words "At meal-time come". Later the same year he was chorus-master *and* tenor in Oxford University Opera Club performances of Gluck's *Iphigénie en Tauride*. I was *in* the chorus and so experienced his gifts at first hand.

Next year the Opera Club tackled *The Trojans* – a very big undertaking – in which the chorus has an important role. Royd, of course, prepared it admirably.

At the time he ran the music at Abingdon Grammar School and the headmaster had agreed that because of his demanding involvement with *The Trojans* he might recruit some extra help in the school – and he brought me in. Awkwardly, I *too* got involved in *The Trojans*. Royd and I shared digs in Abingdon and I shall never ever forget my abject terror when riding pillion on his powerful motorbike after rehearsals in Oxford. He did not hang about.

In 1951 at the Edinburgh Festival I had met and much liked the Serbian interpreter for the Yugoslav Ballet. We kept in touch and she suggested I should visit Yugoslavia. This seemed a good idea and I asked Royd to join me. He was keen and on 10 September 1952 we set out, travelling third class, on the forty-five-hour journey to Belgrade. In the last stages the seats had no upholstery of any kind. But we were royally entertained in Tito's capital – and were embarrassed when bidden to the Opera Director's box for *La bohème* (in Serbo-Croat): anoraks and holiday trousers were our only dress, one rucksack each our only luggage.

The journey over the mountains to Dubrovnik was not without its problems. Arriving very late one night we could find no accommodation, so settled down in the garden of the hotel we had hoped to occupy. My diary records that, "We woke at 5 – or rather, I did, for Royd, by now sleeping on a table, was snoring noisily as the sun rose." A day or two later a party developed with some young Croatians and "we moved to the dining-room, where slivovitz was brought, songs sung and stories told. Soon it was first names all round and a boy called Misko addressed Royd and me indiscriminately as 'Johnnie'."

We voyaged up the coast via Korčula, Hvar, Split, Rab to Rijeka, from where we took a train to Venice. We had swum every day and at Rab I had introduced Royd to maraschino – a welcome change from gut-blistering slivovitz. We had also introduced ourselves to two German girls with whom we spent

181

a jolly evening. Addresses were exchanged but nothing came of either contact as far as I know.

It had been a glorious holiday – and Royd the ideal companion, cheerful and resourceful.

Now our *professions* began to preoccupy us. Royd was of course discretion itself about his work but in about 1973 I *think* I tripped over a trace of it. Walking to the BBC I came across Royd on Primrose Hill and he was *loitering* – which was uncharacteristic. He was friendly, but evasive – so I went on my way, fantasising about a John le Carré scenario.

It is in musical contexts, though, that I shall best remember him. He was a born choral conductor, his movements elegant and expressive, his vocal illustrations always helpful. And he was helpful in other ways. In 1954 I had conducted Handel's *Semele*. Royd, playing oboe, and Felicity viola were in the orchestra and after the first rehearsal he gently reminded me that the right arm should go *up* on the last beat of the bar and *down* on the first.

We also sometimes went to the Hostel of God, a hospice on Clapham Common, where we variously sang and played to the residents, the two Brahms songs with viola among our repertoire.

This was one of Royd's absolutely typical initiatives. He was in every sense a *good* man, a good musician and a good friend.

* * * * *

# 4 – Joe Coolidge

He was, properly speaking, Joseph Randolph Coolidge IV. His wife was the composer-pianist Peggy Stuart. They had a brownstone house in the 50s on New York's East Side and there they generously entertained me when I lived in N.Y. in 1961.

Peggy was pretty and vivacious. And she was a good professional composer of light music; Richard Addinsell might have been an English equivalent, though she never wrote anything as popular as the *Warsaw Concerto*. But her music was not negligible: she had played at the Boston Pops and during the '60s and '70s Joe arranged tours for her in the U.S. and in Europe, even behind the Iron Curtain. When I joined the BBC in 1972 he asked me if I could secure her BBC dates and I tried, but unsuccessfully: Radio 2 – the right place for her music – was not in my gift.

Joe, who married Peggy in 1952, was an unusual personality. He wore a full beard and spoke in what can only be described as a low growl. Such was his modesty that it was years before I discovered that he had been in some covert branch of the Army and that his patrol had been ambushed by the Viet Cong near Saigon. "I was hit with a load of bird-shot in the left arm and in the chest. About half of my triceps were taken away. A second shot with a soft-nosed bullet nicked an artery and took away one half of my vocal cords. To this day I have pieces of the bullet in my throat and have always spoken hoarsely. I also have about 70 pieces of bird-shot in my chest." So he later wrote.

For his services in Viet Nam he was awarded the first Purple Heart of that war. For his services in the Chinese, Burmese and Indian theatres he received the Bronze Star and the Croix de Guerre. He was a very brave man.

Peggy's music apart, the two of them – after Joe's long convalescence – devoted themselves to ecological issues and Peggy often gave her services, once performing at a charity gala arranged by Prince Bernhard of the Netherlands, who was then prominent in the World Wildlife Fund. They came regularly to Europe (Joe loved to travel) and generally passed through London, so that I was able to keep up with them. On one such visit in the late '70s they told me that she had cancer. "The prognosis is not good," Peggy added. She died in 1981 and soon afterwards Joe built himself a small log house overlooking a peaceful lake in New Hampshire. He continued to come to London and once brought with him an erstwhile colleague from the Office of Strategic Services, what we would call Special Operations. She was Barbara Podoski, of whom Joe said, "There is a good chance Peggy had something to do with our meeting again." In any case, Joe and 'Zuzka', who was originally Czech and passionately interested in Janáček's music, became devoted partners (both were pious), spending time together both in Joe's log house and in her home in Washington D.C.

Joe died after heart surgery in his early 80s. No doubt well-to-do, he led a life of generous modesty, much more concerned for the welfare of others than of himself. And he had a nice sense of humour. At Christmas 1987 he sent me a photo of himself kneeling to examine the hand of a smallish, cage-free ape. The inscription read:

For unalloyed affection you can't beat the maidens of Borneo.
We wish you abundant bananas for the holidays and 1988.
With affectionate regards
Grace and Joe

Perhaps I can come to London in late spring – if Grace doesn't claim me.

\* \* \* \* \*

# 5 – Colin Davis

On 22 April 2013 I went to the Festival Hall to hear Imogen Cooper in Beethoven's First (actually second) Concerto. The performance was very enjoyable, the last movement irresistibly bubbly and fast. Afterwards I went down to see Imogen, but found I was not on a list of authorised visitors. I had begun to protest rather pompously when Mitsuko Uchida – whom I did not know – emerged from the sanctum which I wanted to enter. When she saw me she gave me an impulsive hug and thanked me effusively for my obituary of Colin Davis (*The Independent*, 16 April 2013). Here it is:

On 4 February 1950, in the Holywell Music Room at Oxford, Colin Davis conducted *Don Giovanni* for the Chelsea Opera Group.* He was 22. I was the Masetto and was either adequate or beyond hope, for almost all that Colin said to me at rehearsal, apropos the start of the Act 1 Finale, was, "You will sound really angry, won't you?" The performance, whatever its failings had one shining virtue: Davis's passionate commitment to the score and the combination of energy and intellect which he brought to it.

At the time he described himself as living in the "freelance wilderness", and nothing much was to change for seven years. But after the *Don Giovanni* people began to talk: here was a remarkable talent, though one handicapped by the fact that he was not a pianist.

This meant that one of the best ways of becoming a conductor, by serving as repetiteur in an opera house, was closed to him. But he was a good clarinettist, having won a scholarship to the Royal College of Music from Christ's

---

* On 18 June 2000 there was a 50th Anniversary Reunion performance, which Colin Davis conducted. Roderick Williams was the Don; David Cairns (originally Leporello) and I were in the chorus.

Hospital. He played when and where he could, most notably for the great Fritz Busch at Glyndebourne, offstage in *Don Giovanni* and in the pit in *Così fan tutte*. And after service as a bandsman in the Household Cavalry he was asked to conduct the Kalmar Orchestra, a group of students at the Royal College who wanted to get to know the orchestral repertoire. From this grew the Chelsea Opera Group – and the Oxford *Don Giovanni*.

Among those who heard rumours of his gifts were Bernard Robinson and William Glock. Robinson's Music Camp and Glock's summer school at Bryanston afforded chances to conduct. At Bryanston in 1951 he discovered Berlioz – "one of the most marvellous moments of my life" – and Stravinsky. But still there was no breakthrough and the middle '50s were tough. In 1949 he had married the soprano April Cantelo and she was effectively the breadwinner, an arrangement no doubt irksome to someone as self-sufficient as Davis.

The tide began to turn in 1957 when his third application for the post of assistant conductor of the BBC Scottish Orchestra was successful. He had not worked much with professionals and was not familiar with their 'language' and how to get the best out of them. In Glasgow he could make his mistakes and learn his lessons in relative obscurity. He learned fast, but he was not yet confident of his own authority and could be surly and abrupt. By all accounts the musicians were patient.

The year 1959 brought him success on a scale to match his ability. Replacing Klemperer with the Philharmonia he had accompanied Clara Haskil admirably, and I suggested he should appear at the Edinburgh Festival (which I was directing) with the London Mozart Players. He gave memorably mature performances of Stravinsky's *Danses Concertantes* and the 'Jupiter' Symphony and Peter Heyworth, in *The Observer*, described him as "probably the best we have produced since

Sir Thomas Beecham"; it was no doubt this acclaim which persuaded Walter Legge, then running the Philharmonia, to let him loose on a concert performance of *Don Giovanni*, which was a triumph.

Colin Davis had 'arrived' but, ever uncertain of himself, declared that he "wasn't ready to be the kind of success I was supposed to be". (He had once written to Adrian Boult to apologise for an apparent lack of responsiveness on the grounds that "I was not then ready to learn all that you were able to teach me.") It was fortuitous that in the same year he was offered a job with Sadler's Wells (now English National Opera), of which he became Musical Director in 1961.

At the Wells he could do more or less what he wanted and, though he was not consistently successful, there were notable productions – Stravinsky's *Oedipus Rex* and *The Rake's Progress*, *Idomeneo* and *Fidelio* among them. He raised the company's musical standards and discovered the pleasures of working as a team, with Glen Byam Shaw and Norman Tucker. "I learned how to behave myself at Sadler's Wells," he remarked, though not everyone would have agreed with him.

When he left Sadler's Wells in 1964 he became Chief Conductor of the BBC Symphony Orchestra – "the greatest challenge of my life and the completion of my professional education". Relations with the Orchestra were initially difficult. They resented his youth and some disliked his intensity and tendency to philosophise about the music. But he established his authority and the relationship began to pay dividends. Overseas tours followed and there were fine recordings including the Mozart *Requiem*, Haydn's *The Seasons*, *Idomeneo* and *Figaro*, and a string of piano concertos with Stephen Bishop (now Kovacevich), with whom he shared a temperament both serious-minded and mischievous.

He was also a guest with the Boston Symphony and the New York Philharmonic in 1968; a year later he had successes with *Peter Grimes* and *Wozzeck* at the Met. He was appearing regularly at the Royal Opera House, giving *The Trojans* (1969), *Fidelio, Wozzeck* and Tippett's *The Midsummer Marriage*. Tippett found him "the ideal interpreter" and was to dedicate *The Ice Break* (1977) to him. The two had a similar cast of mind, eccentrically philosophic with a vein of quirky, juvenile humour.

When Georg Solti left Covent Garden in 1971 Davis was the obvious successor and reigned there as Music Director for fifteen years. In Götz Friedrich he found a congenial, if controversial, collaborator and their *Ring* cycle, concluded in 1976, was so successful that Davis was invited to open the 1977 Bayreuth Festival, with *Tannhäuser*, the first British conductor to appear there.

The early 1980s were difficult for the Royal Opera House. Hand-to-mouth subsidy caused cancellations, and there were unexpected disappointments. Davis attracted some of the censure and there were signs that his health might be suffering. In November 1984 he wrote that, "internally I am often more depressed than is comfortable". But his second marriage, in 1964, to Ashraf Naini – 'Shamsi' – brought him the most devoted, steady support. A letter about Tippett's Triple Concerto, premiered in 1980, ended, "Shamsi is certainly a gift – in many ways. In any case she's claiming all the honours – for having so many children!"

There were five and they gave him intense happiness. I remember visiting him after the birth of the latest one and his pride when he brought to show me, with loving hands, the tiny, naked person. Years later he was to learn the viola in order to be able to play chamber music with them. He brought them up to love music, to read, enjoy the countryside and to respect animals (there were pet snakes, freely handled, in the household), above all to be "useful". It concerned him deeply that they would grow up in a world apparently in moral and ethical decline.

During his tenure at Covent Garden Davis had attracted a number of appointments, among them Principal Guest with the Boston Symphony (1972–84). He later had a satisfying relationship with the Concertgebouw. He derived special pleasure from the Orchestra of Bavarian Radio, of which he was Principal Conductor from 1983 to 1992, and from the Dresden Staatskapelle, of which he became Honorary Conductor in 1990.

Since 1975 he had been Principal Guest with the London Symphony Orchestra and in 1995 became the more than worthy successor to Michael Tilson Thomas as Chief Conductor. The appointment was astute: Davis had gravitas; his range was enormous; he was relatively young; and seemed to be getting better and better.

His relationship with the LSO was richly productive. In 1995 he led the LSO Tippett Festival, then inaugurated his tenure with Berlioz's *Romeo et Juliette*, adding *La damnation de Faust*, *Harold en Italie* and the *Symphonie fantastique* in overpowering performances for the Bicentenary in 2003. In 2007 he was succeeded by Valery Gergiev but retained the Laureateship of the Orchestra.

In 2010 his wife, Shamsi, died of cancer. He was distraught, and was diagnosed with a minor heart condition. Then came a fall in the pit at Covent Garden, where he was conducting *Die Zauberflöte*. At 83 there was concern about his health. But he was by no means on his last legs. When he left Covent Garden, in 1986, he wrote to me, "I hope you enjoy *Fidelio* – I am privately delighted it has caused such a stir… Better to go out as I came in: unreliable and with an open mind."

This was typical. He was wryly aware of his anarchic streak. No respecter of persons, he detested hypocrisy and pomposity. He was unconventional to the point of childishness, once sticking out his tongue when booed at Covent Garden. But these very characteristics were part and parcel of his "open mind". They ensured that he never sank into a routine and that what he did was always fresh. Moreover, he fed his imagination on the visual arts and on literature: William Blake's drawings and Kazantzakis's *Odyssey* were particular favourites.

He was never less than masterly in Mozart, Beethoven, Berlioz, Sibelius, Tippett, Haydn, Brahms, Wagner and Stravinsky. Late in his career he produced an unforgettably powerful Walton First Symphony and a fine cycle of the Nielsen symphonies. And he was generous towards students, often conducting at the Royal Academy and the Guildhall School, achieving results better than seemed possible.

To everything he did he brought immense – some said too much – energy. He once referred to "the importance of retaining one's sexual capacity". And there was without doubt an erotic element in the way he could, when appropriate, caress a phrase or build a climax. But the physicality of his music-making was counter-balanced by an intellectual rigour. This sometimes resulted in ponderous tempi, but it gave his interpretations a feeling of powerful control and a fine sense of the architecture of the music.

He never lost his respect for great music, particularly the Missa Solemnis (including a magisterial performance at the 2011 Proms), "the last Gothic vision – equal to Chartres or whatever your favourite building – and it embraces everything. I just wish that afterwards I didn't feel such a pretentious worm." Nor did he lose a proper sense of inadequacy. He even retained some bad habits from his youth – "singing along" and mouthing "pom-pom-pom". But they were tiny human flaws and did not prevent him from being showered with prizes and honours.

190

Colin Davis was unaffected by success and was so little interested in what was written about him – or in power for its own sake – that he would have no newspaper or periodical in his house. He guarded the privacy of his family life and to be admitted to it, even a little, was a privilege matched only by the pleasure of observing, over more than sixty years, the development of a towering musical personality. As time went by his progress on to the platform became more stately, his bow more dignified and, towards the audience, deferential. But he retained a positively childlike wonder at the unfathomable potency of great music.

# 27

## Late Days

Though once much influenced by Forster I have recently neglected his advice about the importance of continuing to play the piano. When I last tried I was so disgusted by what I heard that I closed the lid and have not opened it for more than a year. But of course I have continued to listen and a rough, much abbreviated indication of my tastes – which have hardly changed since 1996 when I divulged my Private Passions on Radio 3 – may be gleaned from the list of works I chose:

Brahms: Liebeslieder Waltzes Nos 1–6
Beethoven: Diabelli Variations – No. 24, Fughetta
Mozart: Don Giovanni – Quartet, 'Non ti fidar'
Stravinsky: The Fairy's Kiss – Pas de deux
Schubert: Abendbilder
Janáček: a movement from Mládí
Albéniz: Triana (from Iberia)
Verdi: Falstaff – end of Act 1, Scene 1

Brahms's *Liebeslieder* (their proper title) deserve a chapter to themselves, so remarkable are the names of some of the musicians who, in my time, have sung or played these genial, unbuttoned love-songs. I think of the singers Irmgard Seefried, Kathleen Ferrier, Felicity Lott, Peter Pears, Julius Patzak, Peter Schreier and Dietrich Fischer-Dieskau; the pianists Clifford Curzon, Hans Gál, Claudio Arrau and – astonishingly – Benjamin Britten, well known not to have much liked Brahms's music. His wonderful gifts as an accompanist are more evident in Schubert's *Abendbilder*, and Peter Pears is of course on his own. Whether Britten knew or admired Schnabel's Beethoven I have been unable to discover, but he must surely have appreciated the serene beauty of the Fughetta, the twenty-fourth of the Diabelli Variations, which I heard Schnabel play in the Albert Hall in 1947 and which were on my piano for many years, never completely mastered. The twelve pieces which comprise Albéniz's *Iberia* seem to me to establish their composer as a major contributor to the piano repertoire, comparable to Chopin in his Mazurkas and Polonaises. Less pianistic than Chopin's, Albéniz's writing is formidably difficult, but mastered with panache by Alicia de Larrocha. If Chopin and Albéniz wrote perceptibly Polish and Spanish music, Tchaikovsky's piano-writing is not so obviously 'Russian' (Schumann a frequent influence) and Stravinsky's own unobtrusive Russian-ness combine to make an enchanting ballet score, *Le baiser de le fée*, conducted with love by the composer's friend Ernest Ansermet.

My passion for Janáček's music has been more public than Private: I find that during my tenure of the Proms job I scheduled twenty performances of his works, among them three of the *Glagolitic Mass*. I was proud of all of these, as I was of the award of the Czech Government's Janáček Medal (which is now lodged in the British Museum along with similar 'medals' celebrating 150 years of Vienna's Hofmusikkapelle, the centenary of Szymanowski's birth, Sweden's Royal (Opera) Theatre, Toronto's Mendelssohn Choir and the Leslie Boosey Award, a lovely, chunky disc designed by Elisabeth Frink).

Conspicuously *not* deserving a medal of any kind was Arnold Schoenberg, who described Verdi's *Falstaff* as "... just the sort of stuff a decrepit old man *would* write". Well... that says a very great deal about Schoenberg's judgement – and about his sense of humour, for the opera, unique in Verdi's output (though not in deriving from Shakespeare) is miraculously witty and, as a piece of theatre, is actually better than *The Merry Wives of Windsor*, in which it largely originates. Boito and Verdi together created a master-work, its ensembles comparable with Mozart's in characterisation and mood, 'Non ti fidar', from *Don Giovanni*, providing the divine Sena Jurinac (Donna Elvira) with a fine opportunity to combine dramatic conviction and beauty of sound. I couldn't possibly do without either Falstaff or the Don, however deserted and primitive the island on which I might find myself washed up.

Other must-haves would include Schumann's piano music, preferably played by Imogen Cooper, and Chopin's, with Murray Perahia; Beecham's *Zauberflöte* (with the Berlin Philharmonic), Boult's Schubert 'Great' C major Symphony, Wand's Bruckner 8 and Walton's Violin Concerto, in which the first entry of the soloist – Heifetz of course – matches the same point in Sibelius's concerto, unheralded, adventitious and enchanting. Finally – and there's no more room on my raft – Pierre Boulez's *Rituel: in memoriam Bruno Maderna*. I briefly knew (he was already very ill) and very much liked Maderna and I found touching Boulez's spontaneous and never-revised tribute to a friend and colleague. Pierre, a very important musician and a wholly admirable human being is now (as I write, in August 2015) an ailing 90-year-old, whose friendship I treasure.

I assume Pierre to be an atheist, though I once remarked that in early middle age he was becoming quite a romantic – to which he replied, "Eez nevair too late". So perhaps… But my own position – that of an Anglican agnostic – has to be some kind of a fudge. Nevertheless, I do not believe in an afterlife, but in oblivion. So I shall be oblivious of the further awfulness of Islamist extremism, the miseries of mass migration, the likelihood of cataclysmic climate change, life lived on the internet, robots, the heartless cupidity of 'western' society and of individuals (including bankers) within it and the subhuman nastiness of men like Mugabe and Assad.

But I shall also, alas, be oblivious of friends and relations and nice neighbours, of physical pleasures and visual delights, of landscape, mountains and clouds (including Constable's), of sunshine and warmth, the sound of winds and waterfalls, the calls of birds. Worst of all – but of course oblivion is total, so it won't matter – oblivious of 'classical' music, mankind's supreme achievement in the world of sound – and Beethoven, its supreme practitioner.

# ACKNOWLEDGEMENTS

I am extremely grateful to David Harman, who has typed and computerised this book with a fastidious concern for accuracy which has left me in awe.

And to the friends who encouraged me to start again after the loss of the original script.

# INDEX

This index includes some names which do not occur in the pages of this book. Most obviously, references to *The Trojans* or *The Marriage of Figaro*, for example, are included under Berlioz or Mozart, respectively, whether or not the names of those composers are stated. Similarly, a reference to choreographer Ninette de Valois's ballet *The Rake's Progress* will also earn an entry for its composer, Gavin Gordon; and mention of Baron Ochs will give Richard Strauss (in whose opera *Der Rosenkavalier* the character appears) another page number.

Printed in Great Britain
by Amazon